Toys: Celebrating 100 Years of the Power of Play

T O

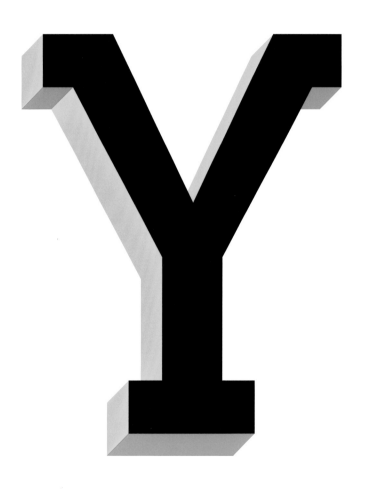

Toys:
Celebrating
100 Years
of the Power
of Play

Written by
Chris Byrne

Foreword by
Judy Ellis

Designed by
Pentagram

Published
by Toy Industry
Association, Inc.

First published in the United States of America in 2003
by Toy Industry Association, Inc.
1115 Broadway
New York, NY 10010

© Toy Industry Association, Inc. 2003

TOY FAIR and AMERICAN INTERNATIONAL TOY FAIR are
trademarks of Toy Industry Association, Inc.

ISBN 0-9726963-1-8

Printed and bound in the U.S.A.

Written by Chris Byrne
Designed by Michael Bierut and Sunnie Guglielmo, Pentagram
Photo research by Janice Carapellucci, Carapellucci Design
Printed by Finlay Printing

Contents

Foreword
The Power
of Play

Judy Ellis
Founder and Chairperson
Toy Design Department
Fashion Institute of Technology
New York City
February 2003

lay is the essential joy of childhood. In this precious time, spontaneous acts reveal new worlds: Window curtains become the entrance onto a stage, and following the path of a caterpillar along the ground can occupy an entire afternoon. I remember so vividly one morning when I spied my niece playing in the kitchen; she watched, fascinated, as boats turned and slowly maneuvered the harsh seas of the sink. Her imagination spun tales of adventure, enthusiastically acted out with miniature yachts improvised from walnut halves she had collected in the backyard. They were simple, yet they floated wonderfully, and that was all that mattered.

Toys can open the door to children's unique and expansive imaginations, places in which they are lost to everything but the moment. When engrossed in play, children are given the opportunity to interact with their surroundings in ways that encourage personal, intellectual and emotional growth. Individual play enables a child to enjoy an intense, intimate world of his or her own making, while group play allows the child to share this interior world with others.

Games provide a unique form of group play. Whether simple or structured, a game lays out a different sort of narrative: like a story, it has a beginning, middle and end. There is dramatic tension as a player takes risks and excitedly anticipates the outcome. When a family plays a game together, a second purpose is served: the chaotic energy of the household is galvanized into one shared activity. The players are allowed to communicate in ways different from their everyday interactions. They compete and strategize, and must react to each other's decisions. Communication among players is encouraged, and the traditional family hierarchy is temporarily leveled. Each player's decision carries equal weight.

Designing a toy is like playing a game of Ping-Pong. On one side of the table is the designer's imagination. On the other side is the designer's understanding of children. The designer strives to make a product that is both creatively satisfying and meets the child's needs. Having the opportunity to incite a moment of discovery—the key to creativity, learning and life—is a gift. Designers educate children by providing them with inventive playthings that excite, inspire, elevate, delight and inform. Children who grow up surrounded by well-designed toys will have higher expectations of their world and of themselves. In this way, designers have an opportunity to contribute to the development of thoughtful, discerning individuals. In order to create toys to meet these standards, designers must have a firm footing in the past and an eye toward the future.

Regardless of what age we live in, a good toy is both timely and timeless. As children grow up, the positive experiences brought about by play affect their way of looking at the world. The bond between a child and a toy can be very powerful, even transforming, as described in the classic children's story *The Velveteen Rabbit*. In one particularly poignant scene, the rabbit wants to understand how to distinguish what is real. "'Real isn't how you're made,' says the Skin Horse. 'It's a thing that happens to you. When a child loves you for a long, long time, not just to play with, but REALLY loves you, then you become Real.'"

The power of the imagination is something that we don't necessarily treasure as children, as it is such an integral part of our childhood. What children take from their experience with toys, after all, is not the memory of the toys themselves, but the reminiscence of individual play experiences called up through their interac-tion with toys—part of a personal mythology that began before they could read or write. As we grow up and our lives become laden with responsibility, taking time to play allows us reentry into life's magic and mystery. When we are aware of possibility, all things are possible: a typewriter gives birth to a book; a blank sheet of paper yields a beautiful musical score. Something as simple as a piece of wood, plastic or fabric transforms into a toy. A walnut becomes a yacht.

A steadfast committee of toy industry pro-fessionals worked for many months to find representative product that reflects design sensitivity, outstanding play value and lon-gevity for inclusion in this wonderful book. The committee deserves much appreciation for the difficult and daunting task of selecting one hundred toys from the innumerable worthy creations produced during the past century. *Toys: Celebrating 100 Years of the Power of Play* could not have been created without this committee, which includes: David Berko, Chris Byrne, Paul Calabro, Diane Cardinale, Daniel A. Chernek, Stan Clutton, Stephanie Janis and Steven Melick. Thanks also go to Michael Bierut, Janice Carapellucci and Sunnie Guglielmo, and special thanks to the Board of Directors and members of Toy Industry Association, Inc.

Introduction

Chris Byrne
New York
February 2003

oday's global toy business is a distinctly twentieth-century invention. The shifts from an agrarian to an industrial and, ultimately, an information-driven society literally created what we call childhood. With the luxury of time and increasing life expectancy, children were free to be children longer and take up adult responsibilities later than ever before.

Yet for all the developments of the past hundred years, one thing remains virtually unchanged: the role of play in the lives of children.

Through play, children explore their worlds and their roles, and begin to see themselves in the context of the culture as a whole. They learn lessons they will need in later life and become familiar with the tools of our culture. So, whether it's a Ma-Ma doll or an advanced chip-driven playmate, the essential play is the same. Toys have always, naturally, reflected their time, and it's important to recall that what seems quaint and antique to us in 2003 was amazing in 1903.

In looking at toys in the twentieth century, there are really four distinct eras, each characterized by decade after decade of innovation, entertainment and fun—simple pleasures for a complex world. While these are not discreet and overlap, they illuminate major trends that have shaped toys and play.

Starting with the growth of manufacturing in the middle of the nineteenth century, iron, wood, paper and composition were the standards of the American manufacturers. The toys were simple games and role-playing items. More elaborate and sophisticated toys came from Europe.

In 1903, the first American Toy Fair trade show took place in New York. American toy companies sought to establish themselves and serve a growing population. Over the next forty years, the toy industry would become more centered in the U.S. Toys would become increasingly sophisticated, but for the most part, a child's world was a literal miniature of an adult's, as it had been through history. But that was about to change.

After World War II, plastics developed for the war effort were turned to peacetime use, including toys. Metal fabrication plants that had been cranking out munitions began to make swing sets and bicycles, which became fixtures on the landscape in booming suburbia. Toys were bigger, brighter and more entertaining.

And then there was television. As TV became a standard appliance in nearly every home, cultural experience was homogenized. We all watched the same things. Children all wanted the same toys. Roy Rogers, Howdy Doody and the Mickey Mouse Club became the shared experience of a generation.

The 1960s and 1970s saw dramatic changes in our culture, a new focus on youth, fun and entertainment, all of which was reflected in toys as more sophisticated design and production helped make them more magical and exciting than ever before.

Starting in the 1980s, technology was one of the major driving forces in our society and the toy industry. That doesn't surprise today's children. They live in a world surrounded by technology; they expect it in toys...and everything else. Yet technology alone does not make a great toy. With more kinds of toys available than at any other time in history, children still naturally gravitate to those toys that engage their imaginations.

And so we end the century where we started. More accurately, toys may have changed, but people haven't. Whether powered by a computer chip or simply a playing card, the most valuable, memorable and important play experiences will be those that inspire an individual child's imagination. At the end of the day, the ability to connect to the imagination will always be what makes a great toy, for it is the imagination that makes us unique creatures and connects us to our past...and our future.

For now, though, let's leave the future to its own devices. Let's look back at this truly remarkable century and some of the toys that shaped our lives.

The watchword as the twentieth century began was progress. The industrial age had finally arrived, and mass production put all kinds of consumer goods into the hands of everyday consumers. Everything was about speed and technology, as it would be for the rest of the century. It was a decade of marvels as motion pictures, radio and the phonograph would become part of the culture, and what people called "modern entertainment" was born.

Gibson girl, c. 1900

The brand new box camera allowed anyone to take snapshots, dispelling the starchy formality of family photos of earlier decades. ■ It was the time of Gibson girls and barbershop quartets, when innocence and new sophistication coexisted. The automobile arrived, with affordable Model T Fords making private transportation more available than ever before. Motoring and speed became passions, and the twenty-mile-per-hour limit seemed dangerously fast to many. Networks of roads began radiating out from the urban centers, and songs like "In My Merry Oldsmobile" celebrated the new sense of freedom that mobility brought. ■ The culture celebrated a brighter, newer and shinier future. In 1904, more

Festival Hall and Central Cascade, St. Louis World's Fair, 1904

1903-1912 A New Century

than twenty million people descended on St. Louis to visit the World's Fair and experience that future full of such wonders as air-conditioning and "fast" food cooked with electricity. Clearly, a new era was dawning, and the Victorian conventions were becoming a thing of the past. ■ The miracles of mass production filled the pages of the Montgomery Ward and Sears Roebuck catalogs. Education became more important and was formalized during this period, and growing affluence planted the seeds of what we consider modern childhood. ■ In business, it was a time of astonishing and exponential growth, with U.S. Steel and Standard Oil virtually indomitable forces. And it was a decade of influential people setting the tone of progress for the remainder of the century. These included President Theodore Roosevelt, who, among his many achievements, created an awareness of the environment and established the national parks. Booker T. Washington and W.E.B. Dubois champion begin the cause of civil rights. John D. Rockefeller, both a captain of industry and a philanthropist, worked to improve education. William

Kodak Box Brownie camera advertisement, c. 1901

Scene from the film *The Great Train Robbery*, c. 1903

Randolph Hearst and Joseph Pulitzer revolutionized journalism and created the modern newspaper. ■ At the beginning of the decade, most entertainment was centered in the home or nearby. Adults sang, read, played card games, dominoes and lotto games, and Parcheesi (though nearly forty years old) was always a favorite. For younger children, there were alphabet books, Noah's Arks, wooden toys and that amazing technology, the Ma-Ma doll, which actually said "Ma-Ma" when turned over. Home train sets had real, miniature steam engines, and Ping-Pong was a nationwide craze. Then, as now, children played what they saw, so the first miniature cars appeared, alongside what we now call role-playing toys—tools, household devices, dollhouses and more. ■ By the end of the decade, mass entertainment would move out of the home with the introduction of the nickelodeon and movies first

Women drivers, c. 1905

shown in small arcades and then moving into full-size theaters. Classics like the 1903 *Great Train Robbery* would introduce the public to this new form of entertainment and would begin the era of experience shared nationwide and the true emergence of a cultural identity. ■ Progress also meant greater affluence and the beginning of a consumer culture. Advertising and compet-

Dancing couple, 1910s

ition boomed as more and more companies began to address the emerging consumer markets. ■ Even in toys. In 1900, many toys sold in the U.S. still came from Europe, and in 1903, hoping to further establish the relatively new American toy industry, manufacturers gathered in New York to attract the attention of store buyers as they departed to and returned from Europe. This showcase, on docks or in offices near the piers, was the first occurrence of what by the end of the century would be known as the American International Toy Fair. It was, to be sure, a modest beginning, yet it was fueled by the hope and confidence that would drive the American toy business for the remainder of the century.

A woman playing lawn croquet, c. 1910

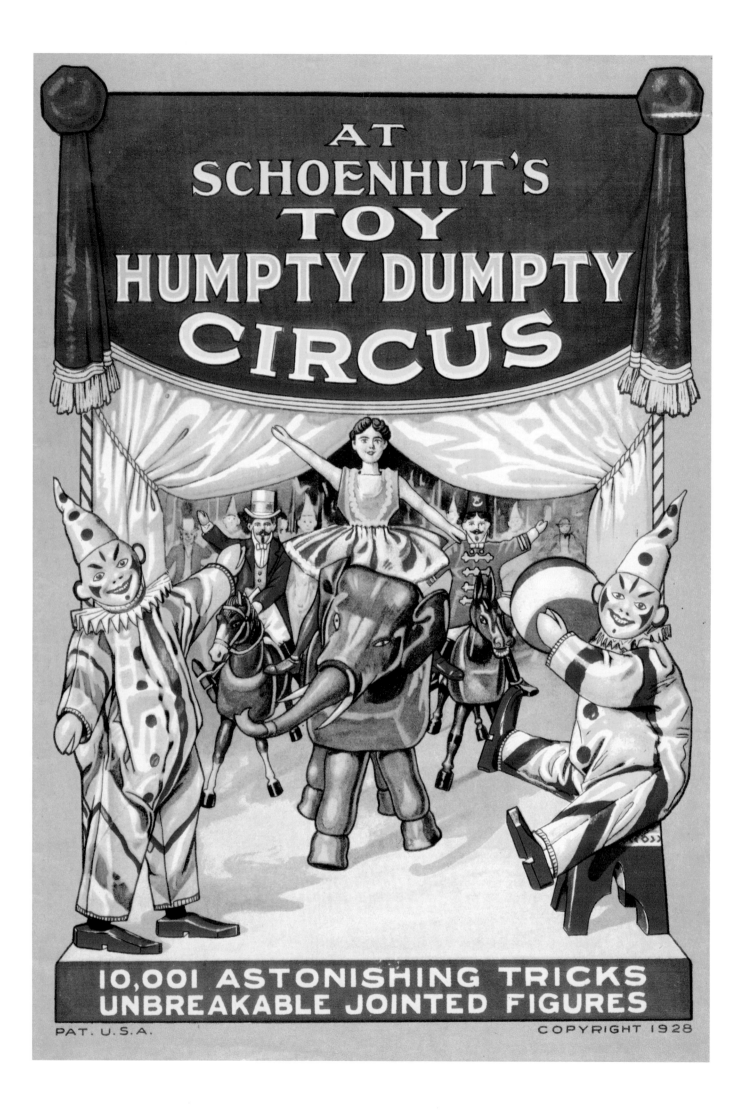

Alfred Schoenhut, a German immigrant, is credited with establishing one of the first American toy factories, in Philadelphia, Pennsylvania, in 1872. The company specialized in wooden toys and pianos, but it was the introduction of the Humpty Dumpty Circus that put Schoenhut's company on the map.

Throughout the nineteenth century, thanks in large measure to P.T. Barnum and others, circuses were a major form of entertainment in the U.S., but until Schoenhut, no one had created a toy inspired by the circus. In fact, Schoenhut really created what we know today as the play set—

a group of integrated characters within an environment. Previously, toy manufacturers had made dollhouses or Noah's Ark sets, but no one had ever created a whole world for children to play with and bring to life with their imaginations.

And what a world! Starting in 1903, Schoenhut introduced clowns, followed in 1904 by more animals and figures. He introduced the tents in 1907, and continued until 1909, populating his circus and sideshow with every imaginable kind of character.

Originally made of wood, the ingenious toys were jointed and could perform all kinds of tricks, allowing kids to pretend they ran the show. In later years, Schoenhut introduced metal characters and tents, adding to the world of his circus, which was manufactured continuously until 1935.

New figures joined the circus every
year…for thirty-two years

1903 Crayola Crayons

A Yale University study ranked Crayola Crayons eighteen on a list of the twenty most recognizable scents to American adults.

Crayons have been a springboard for creative imaginations for more than a century

Today, Binney & Smith estimates that by age six, the average child in the U.S. will have gone through more than 700 crayons. That's a lot of coloring, and crayons remain one of the staples of imagination and childhood.

Binney & Smith began its life in 1880 as a company making pigment—the familiar red oxide of barns and carbon black of tires. (Before Binney & Smith was around, Goodrich's tires had been white.) In 1900, the company branched out, making marking inks and black wax marking pencils, and using the abundant slate in the area of Easton, Pennsylvania, for a new product—slate pencils. The company's next product, dustless chalk, cleaned up schoolrooms forever and won a gold medal at the St. Louis World Exposition in 1902.

But the best was yet to come. In working with teachers, Binney & Smith saw there was also a need for better wax crayons, ones that had more staying power and more color. Adapting the wax marking pencils, the company made them smaller and added a variety of new pigments to the paraffin. In 1903, Binney & Smith produced the first box of eight crayons, which sold for five cents and contained black, brown, blue, red, purple, orange, yellow and green.

But what to call them? Edward Binney's wife, Alice, who was a schoolteacher, found the solution. She took the French word for chalk, *craie,* and combined it with "oleaginous," a now obscure adjective that defined the waxy consistency of the crayons. The result: Crayola...literally "oily chalk."

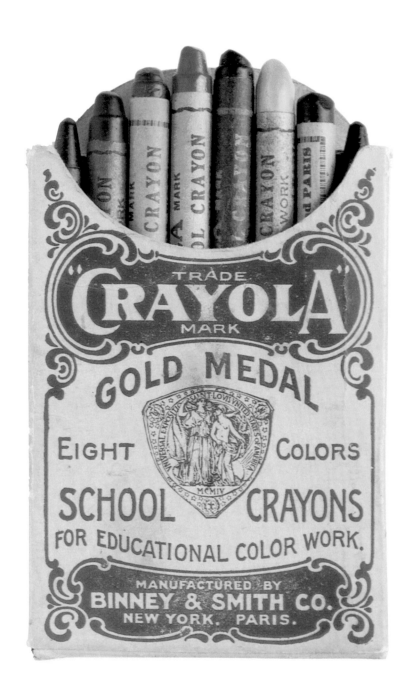

c. 1903
Lionel Trains

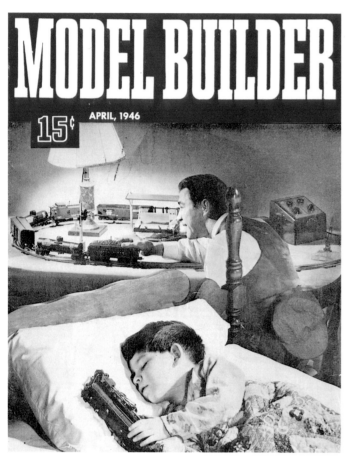

An early electric controller which helped make model railroading available to the general public

Cowen's manufacturing innovations helped create the hobby of model training as we know it today. He was the first to use sheet steel in the manufacture of trains. He created both the "standard gauge" system and what we know today as "O" gauge.

What really distinguished Cowen's creations, though, was the decoration. With more than 35,000 trains running in the U.S. at the time, Cowen painted his cars to resemble the full-size trains riding the rails, and the concept of collectibility was born. Cowen's other innovations included the broad range of accessories that worked with the trains and the first model train transformer, which allowed the power to come from the wall instead of a light socket.

Cowen founded a company that allowed millions of people to live their railroading fantasies in miniature, and he never forgot that what he was making was a toy. Never content to simply have trains run around tracks, Cowen constantly added animated features and unique accessories, beginning a tradition of innovation and fun that continues to this day.

At the beginning of the twentieth century, toy trains were certainly not uncommon in the U.S., whether they were push toys or had real working miniature steam engines. The romance of the train and travel was already deeply ingrained in American culture. No wonder kids loved playing with trains.

Though the first electric train was exhibited at the 1893 Chicago World's Fair, it would be the ingenuity and passion of twenty-two-year-old toy maker Joshua Lionel Cowen that were responsible for one of the most enduring toy brands of all time.

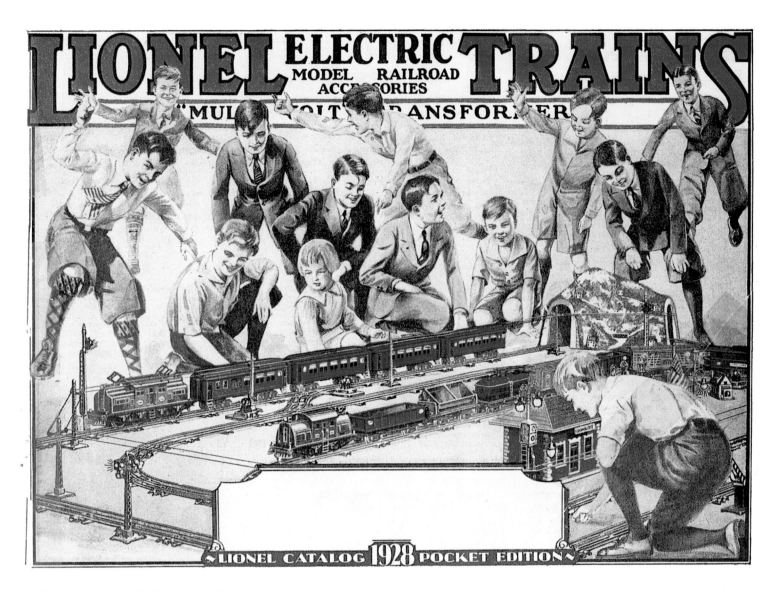

Joshua Lionel Cowen's innovations and introductions helped create the hobby of model railroading.

LIONEL *o* **MINIATURE** *o*

ELECTRIC CA

With full accessories for

WINDOW and **HOLID**
DISPLAY **GIFTS**

LIONEL MFG. CO. N.Y.

MANUFAC

LIONEL MANUFACT

24 and 26 MURRAY STREET,

R S

ED BY

RING CO., Incorporated.

NEW YORK.

1903 Teddy Bear

In 1902, Teddy Roosevelt refused to shoot a bear cub whose mother had been killed in the hunt. The story became nation-wide news and was reflected in a cartoon by Clifford Berryman in *The Washington Post*.

Many people want to lay claim to having originated the Teddy Bear, arguably one of the most popular and enduring toys of the twentieth century. And there are many conflicting stories, each with its passionate adherents. Some say it was named for King Edward VII, who was known as "Teddy." The Steiff Company, one of the largest manufacturers of stuffed toys in England, created a bear in 1903, inspired by sketches of cubs at a local zoo. These toys soon found their way to the U.S.

But easily the most widely accepted story has to do with President Theodore (Teddy) Roosevelt. On a hunting trip in Mississippi in 1902, Roosevelt refused to shoot a bear cub whose mother had been killed in the hunt. As anything a president does is newsworthy and subject to editorializing, the story gained wide circulation and was reflected in a cartoon by Clifford Berryman in *The Washington Post*. Captioned "Drawing the Line in Mississippi," the cartoon soon circulated throughout the nation.

In Brooklyn, Morris Michtom and his wife, Rose, saw the cartoon, and Rose made a bear, which was displayed in the window of their shop with a copy of the cartoon and a sign that said "Teddy's Bear." Soon the Michtoms couldn't keep up demand for the adorable stuffed animals. When Roosevelt, at Michtom's request, granted permission for the use of his name, the Ideal Novelty and Toy Company was born in 1903.

Since then, however it got here, the Teddy Bear has remained one of the most enduring and beloved toys ever created.

"I will build a motorcar for the great multitude," Henry Ford was famous for saying. And he did. Though the Ford Model T was not the first car built in the United States, in 1909 it was the first that was affordable to the average citizen. And over nineteen years, Ford produced more than fifteen million Model T vehicles, transforming the culture and ushering in the modern age.

Not surprisingly, with cars so much on the minds of virtually everyone, it wasn't long before kids were clamoring for their very own Model T vehicles. Samuel Dowst, whose company, Dowst Brothers, made a variety of die-cast fashion and laundry accessories, is credited with creating the first die-cast car in the U.S., launching an enduring sector of the toy industry—and ensuring that toy cars would be part of nearly every childhood from that time forward.

After the launch of his toy Model T vehicle, with the die-cast car business firmly established, Dowst renamed his company "Tootsietoy," in 1924, in honor of his brother's granddaughter. Two years later, the company was acquired by Chicago businessman Nathan Shure's Cosmo Manufacturing Company. At the dawn of the twenty-first century, the Shure family still runs the business, now known as the Strombecker Corporation.

Like Ford, Strombecker's Tootsietoy has delighted the "great multitude," and today produces more than forty million die-cast cars every year.

1910
Ford Model T
Die-cast Car

With the nineteenth century well in the past, a uniquely American cultural identity was emerging as the nation expanded its unique role on the world stage as both an economic and political leader. For the first time, it was the U.S. that was at the forefront of a changing world and, thanks to improved travel, growing affluence and World War I, by the end of the decade the distinct American-style culture would set international trends. ■ America was all

Mary Pickford, 1920

about youth and vigor. Victorian reserve gave way to "pep." From music to entertainment to fashion, everything began to loosen up. Mothers may have been Gibson girls,

but daughters were going to be flappers. Hemlines crept up. No one wanted to look like his stable grandfather; the new ideal was those fun-loving college kids, and you didn't have to go to college to do the varsity drag. ■ American industry was booming, and American-made products were considered the best in the world, and not just at home. Moreover, the growing middle class was more affluent, so these goods were suddenly within the reach of more people, and people began to buy on credit. And

as the nation began the buildup to war, the U.S. became the world industrial leader. ■ The

Sheet music for the song "Hold Me," from the *Zigfield Follies* of 1920

Victrola supplanted the piano in the parlor. Popular music became accessible to millions, and more and more people could afford automobiles. More than

1913-1922 American Culture Emerges

thirty million people went to the movies every week. They watched as Theda Bara vamped her way into the hearts of the nation, while Charlie Chaplin

Times Square at night, 1921

tramped into immortality. There were serials like *The Perils of Pauline*, and Mary Pickford was America's sweethearts just as Douglas Fairbanks was everyone's hero. Dance crazes like the fox-trot and the risqué tango swept the nation. The tango was so suggestive, in fact, that it was banned in Boston, Cleveland and New York. But all this was nothing next to what was becoming the most influential

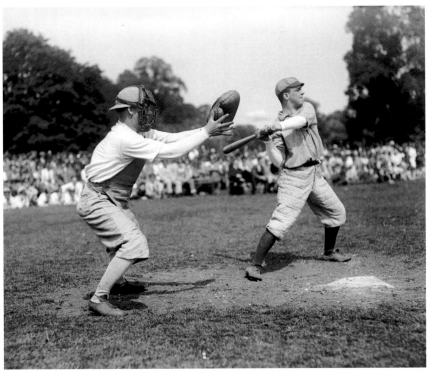
Playing ball, 1917

medium of its time—radio, which began in 1920 when KDKA received the first commercial broadcasting license. ■ Much entertainment was still centered on the home. Grown-ups played parlor games. Lotto was still popular, as were new word or card games, and the Ouija board became quite a fad for a while. People read Edith Wharton, Ezra Pound, T.S. Eliot, Somerset Maugham, H.L. Mencken, D.H. Lawrence, Zane Gray, H.G. Wells and Edgar Rice Burroughs. They listened to the music of Porter, Gershwin, Kern, Berlin and Rodgers, and many of the songs we now consider standards were added to the American songbook. With the war came patriotic songs and, significantly, the exportation of the American sound around the globe. Broadway was booming. To those who remember the time, the atmosphere was almost giddy. ■ Of course, there were challenges. Education, labor, health and Prohibition all captured headlines, as did the suffragist movement and the rights of women, who finally got the vote with the ratification of the Nineteenth Amendment in 1920. Through all of these, for better or worse, the culture was changed forever politically and socially. ■ For children in this booming America, it was the heyday of building toys. Erector Sets, Lincoln Logs and Tinkertoys all made their debuts during this decade. More than fifty million toy Model T Fords were sold, making the nation's fascination with speed child-sized. Dolls continued to be popular as the new, American-made celluloid dolls replaced imported china. ■ It was a time of triumph, tragedy and, most of all, change. The modern world was born, and World War I forced

Charlie Chaplin, c. 1920

Outdoor boxing match between two heavyweight boxers, 1919

America to grow up in a sense, to become wiser and, alongside the frivolity, perhaps a bit more serious. What was also born in this period was the spirit of optimism and enterprise that is distinctly American. Surrounded by it, children were interpreting this spirit in their play, and it would, in part, inspire them to shape the years between the wars.

MANUAL OF INSTRUCTION
PART I

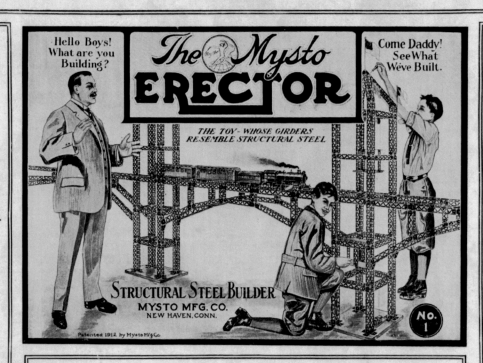

ITS
POPULARITY
IS
THE
WONDER
OF
THE
TOY WORLD

MAKES
MORE MODELS
BUILDS
BIGGER MODELS
HAS
MORE PARTS
FOR YOUR
MONEY
THAN
ANY
SIMILAR TOY

Hello Boys! What are you Building?

Come Daddy! See What We've Built.

The Mysto **ERECTOR**

THE TOY - WHOSE GIRDERS RESEMBLE STRUCTURAL STEEL

STRUCTURAL STEEL BUILDER
MYSTO MFG. CO.
NEW HAVEN, CONN.

NO. 1

Patented 1912 by Mysto Mfg Co

READ
ABOUT
PRIZE
CONTEST
ON
PAGE TWO
SEE
PHOTOS
OF
BOYS
WHO WON
PRIZES

YOU HAVE
THE NEWEST
STEEL
CONSTRUCTION
TOY
OF
THEM ALL
EASIEST
QUICKEST
TO
BUILD
WITH

THE MYSTO MFG. CO., NEW HAVEN, CONN.

PRICES FOR MANUALS: No. 1—15c.; No. 2—15c.; No. 3—15c. ALL POST-PAID

Using the metal pieces, screws and nuts, children could build whatever they imagined.

Inventor A.C. Gilbert said that he was inspired to create the Erector Set by watching men work on building the power line stanchions that lined the train tracks between New York and New Haven. Meccano had already established a market for this kind of toy as one of the earliest metal construction sets, but Gilbert saw greater potential, perhaps because of all the full-scale building taking place in the U.S. in 1913 as the country moved out and up in ways that would have seemed inconceivable a few years earlier.

Gilbert also understood structural engineering, and in designing Erector, he created unique tooling on the sides of his pieces that allowed builders to fit them together to create sturdy, square girders and give a previously unachieved stability to models. Using the metal pieces, screws and nuts, children could build whatever they imagined or could follow the detailed instructions that included such elaborate construction elements as "eccentric motion" mechanisms, wheel bearings and gear-and-pulley brakes.

Under the banner "Hello Boys! Make Lots of Toys," models ranged from simple pushcarts and grindstones to full-scale amusement parks, complete with working rides. The world of Erector reflected the world in which children lived. Right from its launch at the Toy Fair trade show in 1913, Erector allowed children to participate imaginatively in the American building boom.

Over the years, Erector, which was ultimately acquired by Meccano at the end of the century, has changed to reflect the world of each successive generation of kids, but the process of building with real steel and imagination remains unchanged.

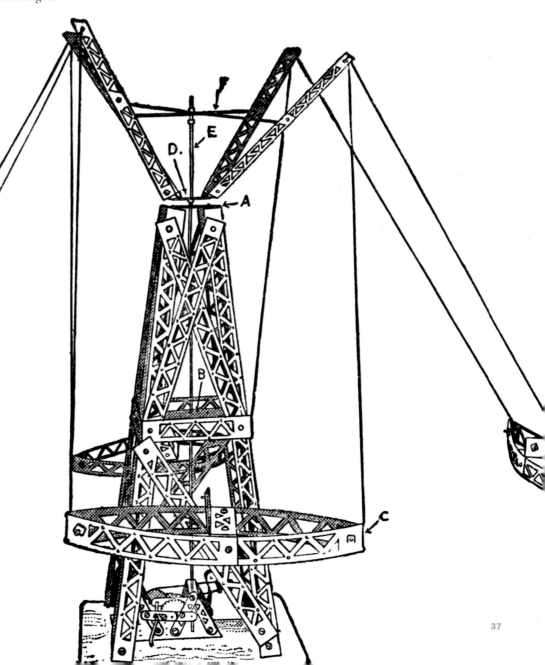

No. 254—Circle Swing

BUILD frame work first. Attach circle plate at (A), another circle plate (D) holding the arms in place with acute and obtuse angles. (F) represents cross girders from which the shafting rod passes down through circle plate (D) through circle plate (A), through base plate (B) connected with couplings down to gear box. For construction see model 176. The gear box is driven by a motor, and the boats (C) when the swing gets in motion, will fly out into the air. This is a very attractive model and works beautifully. Very simple to construct.

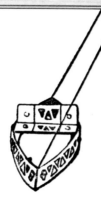

1914
Tinkertoy

"The Wonder Builder" Tinker Toy

One of the cleverest builders toys on the market. Sales are big and profit is good

GYRO TRAVELER
24 INCHES HIGH

WIND MILL
30 IN. HIGH

F3625—"The Wonder Builder" smooth finish turned wood dowels, asstd. lengths, grooved ends, fit in circular hardwood blocks, instruction sheets showing derricks, merry-go-round, elevators, aeroplanes, etc., one set may be added to another to make more elaborate models. Each set in litho box. 1/12 doz. sets in pkg.................Doz. sets, **$6.00**

As has always been the case, it's the imagination, not the objects, that makes an experience fun. So in 1913, as Illinois stonemason Charles Pajeau watched his children thoroughly engrossed in playing with a collection of sticks, pencils and empty spools, he had an idea for a three-dimensional abstract building toy. In his garage, Pajeau milled spools and rods of different lengths and colors, creating a colorful set with just three basic parts that could be assembled in ways limited only by a child's imagination.

It seemed perfect, and convinced from his kids' reaction that he had a hit on his hands, Pajeau took his creation—now called Tinkertoy—to the Toy Fair in 1914. Not a single toy store was interested in carrying his beloved invention, and the idea almost ended there.

But, if the history of toys teaches us anything, it's never to give up on an idea you believe in. Taking on the marketing himself for the holidays in 1914, Pajeau masterminded a stunt: He hired several people, dressed them as elves and set them to work creating with Tinkertoys in the window of Marshall Field's. That was all it took. The story went nationwide and within a year Pajeau had sold more than one million Tinkertoy sets.

Whether Marcella found the doll in her grandmother's attic and brought it to her father or Gruelle found it himself and thought it would make a good story is unclear.

Raggedy Ann dolls were originally hand-made; the newer mass-produced dolls, shown with a loving make-believe mother, would become the classics most people remember

The origin of Raggedy Ann and her brother, Raggedy Andy, is surrounded by legend. Johnny Gruelle was a commercial artist and political cartoonist who refurbished an old rag doll for his beloved daughter, Marcella. (Whether Marcella found the doll in her grandmother's attic and brought it to her father or Gruelle found it himself and thought it would make a good story is unclear.) Gruelle named the doll Raggedy Ann, combining the titles of two poems by his friend James Whitcomb Riley, "The Raggedy Man" and "Little Orphan Annie." What is known is that Marcella loved her doll, and when she died at the age of thirteen from complications from a smallpox vaccination, Gruelle was completely devastated.

The first book of Raggedy Ann stories, published in 1918, was a collection of the stories Gruelle told his daughter as she lay ill. The book was a hit and Marcella was immortalized, through twenty-five books in all, as the little girl whose toys were more than passive playthings; they had *adventures*.

The first Raggedy Ann dolls were created by Gruelle and his family to promote the book. (Gruelle patented the doll in 1918, and his family still holds the patent today.) Some even say that the family stitched real candy hearts into the dolls to match Raggedy Ann's most famous and sweetest characteristic. The first toy company to produce mass-market Raggedy Ann dolls in 1935 was P. F. Volland Exposition Doll and Toy Manufacturing. Subsequently Knickerbocker assumed manufacturing rights, to be followed by Hasbro and Applause.

Ardent collectors, who remain loyal to the doll who always does the right thing, hold onto the legend as much as to their precious collectibles.

1915
Raggedy
Ann
& Andy

1916 Lincoln Logs

As much as they've become associated with the American frontier, largely due to their name and extensive promotion on TV's "Pioneer Playhouse" in 1953, the real inspiration for Lincoln Logs is said to have been a Japanese hotel. John Lloyd Wright maintained that he got the idea to create a building toy as he watched the construction of the Imperial Hotel designed by his father, Frank Lloyd Wright, in Tokyo. The hotel was supposed to be one of the first earthquake-proof buildings ever constructed, and the interlocking logs, which could move with the seismic waves without collapsing and were known as "floating cantilever construction," gave young Wright his idea for the toy.

Wright designed sticks of wood with notches cut in them so the pieces could interlock. He also included architectural details so kids' buildings could be a bit more realistic.

But what about that name—where did it come from? Wright had first made a simple building, and it reminded him of a log cabin, so he named his toy Lincoln Logs in honor of the president born in such a building. As the West was still a source of much fantasy and romance, the name seemed a perfect fit.

First introduced to a broad marketplace in 1924, the toy was a huge success, experiencing several periods of renewed popularity after World War II, in the 1950s and again in the late 1990s.

John Lloyd Wright maintained that he got the idea to create a building toy as he watched the construction of Tokyo's Imperial Hotel designed by his father, Frank Lloyd Wright.

LINCOLN LOGS
AND
ALLIED TOYS FOR CHRISTMAS GIFTS

THERE'S real FUN for the youngsters in these toys. Using LINCOLN LOGS children fashion with their own hands Pioneer Buildings, such as Lincoln's Cabin or Valley Forge. The HISTORICAL FIGURES made of tough metal portray Settlers, Cowboys, Indians, Soldiers of 1812, Sailors and many others.

Take the children to see our exhibits in the stores, including the new BARN SET, the EARLY AMERICAN FORTS, like Fort Dearborn at the World's Fair. Examine the LINCOLN BRICKS which are put together with MORTAR. Our wide selection of unbreakable metal miniatures adds to the play value of all.

PARENTS, if you want your children to play safely and happily at home for hours at a time, get them some of these toys for Christmas and watch them absorb the spirit of Pioneer America.

LINCOLN LOGS and ALLIED TOYS carry the unqualified endorsement of educators and national authorities on Child Welfare.

FORT DEARBORN, the EARLY AMERICAN FORT SETS and the SETTLER'S CABIN are made of LINCOLN LOG LUMBER—several logs in one piece for easy construction.

LINCOLN BARNYARD with 12 Unbreakable Metal Figures, Wooden Barn and 4 Sections of Fence beautifully enameled in Red and Green.

SETS OF UNBREAKABLE METAL FIGURES

If your dealer can not supply you, mail this coupon.

Please order by our Catalogue Number as shown below.

50—Indians.......... 50c	60—U. S. Soldiers of 1918 50c
53—Cowboys Shooting.. 50c	62—Machine Gunners .. 50c
54—Cowboys with Rope. 50c	63—American Sailors... 50c
55—Cowboys and Indians 50c	64—West Point Cadets.. 50c
56—Indians and Pioneers 50c	65—Canadian Police.... 50c
57—Soldiers of 1812.... 50c	70—Farm Set.......... 50c
58—Soldiers of 1776.... 50c	105—Cowboys and Indians
100—Indians, 12 figures.. $1.00	12 figures............$1.00
101—Indians and Pioneers,	110—U. S. Soldiers 1918
14 figures...........$1.00	12 figures............ 1.00
102—Cowboys, 12 figures. 1.00	140—Farm Set with Trees 1.00

The story of the "little red wagon" is a true American story almost as iconic as the Radio Flyer itself. In 1914, sixteen-year-old Antonio Pasin arrived in the U.S. from Italy. His desire to seek his fortune in America was so great that his family had sold their mule to pay for his passage.

Coming from a family of cabinetmakers, Pasin first made wooden wagons in 1917, spending his nights building in a one-room shop. As the business grew, Pasin was able to hire helpers and in 1923, the Liberty Coaster Company was born.

Inspired by the production techniques of the fledgling U.S. auto industry, Pasin switched his construction to metal, turning out a high volume of wagons for the masses and earning himself the nickname "Little Ford."

It would be Model #18, though, that would become the icon and staple of imaginative play and juvenile entrepreneurship. Pasin named his creation Radio Flyer in honor of Americans' fascination with the then brand-new entertainment medium—wireless radio.

Radio Flyer wagons have been continuously produced since then, pausing only during World War II as the company turned its attention to manufacturing the "Blitz Can," an essential tool for mobile artillery units in Europe, Africa and the Pacific.

In the twenty-first century, Radio Flyer is still a mode of transport and a platform for the imagination, and the Pasin family is still creating American dreams for families.

1917 Radio Flyer

Pasin named his creation Radio Flyer in honor of Americans' fascination with the then brand-new entertainment medium— wireless radio.

The giant Radio Flyer would become a staple promotional vehicle for the ever-more popular wagons

1920s
Marbles

Where do you really put marbles in an historic context? We know they go back as far as there is recorded history and most likely before. After all, the first Homo sapiens who played with small rocks could be said to have been playing marbles. Since marble, the material, might not have been discovered or named at the time, they were just round stones.

Like many toys that go in and out of fashion, marbles have enjoyed numerous peaks over the years, but one of the first big crazes for marbles in the U.S. happened in the 1920s. What distinguished the marbles of the 1920s was that for the first time they were being machine made in a wide variety of materials including steel, onyx, agate and what most people today think of: glass. Previously, marbles had been made by hand, either of glass or, very often, fired clay.

Playing "keepsies" was the most heartbreaking game of all because if your opponent won, he got to keep all of your marbles.

In the 1920s and beyond, kids collected marbles and played with them in a variety of ways, often becoming school-yard sharpies with their highly developed styles—dropping, rolling, throwing and shooting (the marble nestled in curled fingers and flicked by the thumb) were all popular. There were also a seemingly endless number of different games, and people who played marbles in the '20s recall having their favorites for luck or performance, which were especially useful when one played "keepsies." Of course, there were always sore losers who were likely to be upset, giving rise to the phrase "to lose one's marbles" as an expression of distress.

In the marble crazes of the '40s and '60s, Cat's Eye marbles and marbles with swirled colored glass inside were all the rage. In the 1960s, there was even a craze for "fried marbles." Marbles were heated in a pan and dropped in ice water to create internal cracking.

Today, you'll find marble players and collectors in virtually every culture around the world. Aeons from now, humans will probably still be fascinated by them.

James Hall, American leading man of the early talkie period, playing marbles on the film lot with some colleagues, namely Louise Brooks, Nancy Phillips, Doris Hill and Josephine Dunn, 1927

With the privations of World War I behind it and its place as a world leader firmly established, America was ready to cut loose. Even the continuing Prohibition couldn't stop people from having a good time. The average workweek had dropped from sixty to forty-eight hours and by and large, as had happened in the previous decade, people had more money to spend and every intention of having a good time. ■ This was the decade of crazy excesses—from dance marathons, some lasting as long as twenty-two weeks, to flagpole sitting to dancing the Charleston. Much of popular culture was focused on youth, fun and exuberance, which continued to find expression in what some older folks thought were increasingly outlandish activities. Promotion and thrill-seeking became the name of the game, and youthful rebellion took the shape of scandalous outfits, the wearing of rouge, eyeliner and nail polish and the rise of the flapper and a new aesthetic in style. ■ As would happen after other wars throughout the century, new technologies found peacetime applications that transformed the culture. In this decade, modern, mass communication was born. Radio, as a source of news and free entertainment, swept the country,

bringing with it the first mass-market advertising. ■ Men and women alike fell in love with movie stars, women swooning

Jazz girls, 1930

Gertrude Ederle, the first woman to swim the English Channel, 1926

over Rudolph Valentino and Rudy Vallee, and men falling for the "It" girl, Clara Bow, the first cinematic sex symbol. Talkies arrived in 1926, with famous stage actor John Barrymore playing Don Juan, and sound cartoons from a young man named Walt Disney (among others) soon followed. Broadway

1923-1932 The Beginnings of Mass Culture

reached an all-time peak with the premieres of *Showboat* by Kern and Hammerstein and many other plays and musicals. ■ Professional sports were firmly established as entertainment in 1920s. The Red Sox sold Babe Ruth to New York, helping create the most famous team of all time—the 1927 Yankees. Professional football, golf, tennis and boxing all entertained legions of fans with their stars, Dempsey, Rockne, Gehrig and others becoming national heroes. ■ On May 21, 1927, Lindbergh completed his solo nonstop transatlantic flight,

Charles Lindbergh flies over the Atlantic, 1927

ushering in the era of commercial aviation. Admiral Byrd flew over the North and South poles, and Niels Bohr discovered the atom. The Pharaoh's tombs were opened in Egypt. Charles Jenkins transmitted the first television images in 1923. It was also a time of great national pride, and Congress concurred, naming "The Star Spangled Banner" the national anthem in 1931. ■ Meanwhile, for those not swallowing goldfish or dancing the night away, the home became a new focus of attention. New appliances (refrigerators, pop-up toasters) joined new

A family gathers around the wireless to hear the daily news, 1931

food technologies (frozen vegetables, thanks to Clarence Birdseye, breakfast cereals, candy bars, prepackaged ice cream), and a period of cozy domesticity prevailed. ■ Improved communication meant that for the first time toys and games could become national fads very quickly. Crossword puzzles became a rage, and everyone, it seemed, was playing an Americanized version of mah-jongg. ■ The automobile was still relatively new, particularly in the mass culture, so toy cars—made of steel windups from companies like Kingsbury Manufacturing—let kids imagine themselves on the

F. Scott Fitzgerald, c. 1930

roads. Dollhouses from Tootsietoy were favorites. This was also the decade that saw two crazes for classic toys—marbles and yo-yos—and Kewpie dolls made their debut. Beatrice "Madame" Alexander began her doll business in 1923 at a kitchen table—a business that would transform the global doll industry. And the modern licensing business was born as a newly introduced character, a mouse named Mickey, appeared in his first cartoon and on a variety of products. ■ It was a shining time for literature as well, with expatriates of the Lost Generation writing in Europe, including Gertrude Stein, F. Scott Fitzgerald and Ernest Hemingway. The Algonquin Round Table met every week in New York City, and African-American authors were heard in numbers for the first time in a move-

Teens skipping rope on the beach, 1925

ment called the Harlem Renaissance. ■ It was a decade often bursting with confidence, optimism and energy. It was the decade of skyscrapers, including the Woolworth Building in New York and the Wrigley Building in Chicago. America's golden future seemed secured. But the decade would hit disaster on October 24, 1929. Forever remembered as Black Thursday, it was the day the stock market crashed, closing the banks and causing a panic on Wall Street. ■ It was the singular event that shaped the rest of this decade and the next, touching every part of the culture.

Fletcher Henderson's orchestra, featuring Henderson, Louis Armstrong, Coleman Hawkins, Buster Bailey and Don Redman, New York City, c. 1924

Pretty soon, kids and adults everywhere were trying to "walk the dog," "rock the baby" or make their yo-yos go "around the world."

Yo-yos have been around pretty much as long as there have been people...and string. They have been found with mummies in the Pyramids, in ancient China and on classic Greek vases—just three examples. Originally made of terra-cotta or wood, or simply rocks with string tied to them (for hunting), they are one of the most rudimentary and, obviously, enduring toys of all time. Over its lifetime the yo-yo has been called "quiz," "bandalore" and "jou jou."

What we think of as the modern yo-yo, however, really only dates back to 1928, when a Filipino named Pedro Flores started selling hand-carved, wooden yo-yos from the Santa Monica hotel where he worked as a bellhop. He even gave the toy its current name, which means "come come" in Tagalog. What made Flores's toys different was that he had invented a string that looped around the dowel holding the two halves of the toy together, so for the first time a yo-yo could "sleep." It was Flores's ability to do tricks with this new yo-yo that attracted the attention of Donald Duncan, who introduced Good Humor Ice Cream. Duncan purchased the toy and the name and set to work popularizing it. Over the next thirty years, he sent out legions of yo-yoers to promote the activity, and the yo-yo experienced several crazes during the twentieth century.

Duncan is also credited with encouraging the development of all the elaborate tricks that separate the really accomplished yo-yoer from the idle player.

1928
Yo-Yo

1930
Mickey and
Minnie

Back in 1928, there were only a few licensed characters, such as Mutt & Jeff and the Yellow Kid, as well as toys based on Western heroes, Bible stories and literature, but character licensing certainly wasn't the global enterprise it is today. That all changed in 1928 with the first synchronized sound cartoon. (For the first time in a cartoon the sound matched the action.) Called *Steamboat Willie*, it was produced by Walt Disney and introduced the character of Mickey Mouse. It was a revelation. Here at last was a charming character that kids could relate to and who consistently made them laugh. The character, a singing, dancing, good-natured mouse, was like nothing anyone had seen before.

In 1930, Disney was convinced that there was an opportunity to sell children's products with the image of the popular character. The first Mickey Mouse licensed product had been a child's writing tablet. Based on its success, Walt Disney had Charlotte Clark design the first Mickey doll, and it was an instant hit. Like many of the stuffed toys of the period, these were more fabric sculptures, great to play with and an accurate representation of the character as seen on the screen. A stuffed version of Minnie soon followed, and two years later, Disney signed a deal with Herman Kay Kamen, and the modern licensing business was born. Mickey and Minnie were followed into products by the whole family of Disney characters, whose enduring appeal has yet to be matched by any other characters.

Seventy-five years later Mickey remains an iconic representation of fun and magic. This is one mouse everyone always wants to have around the house.

1931 Scrabble

Like many overnight sensations, Scrabble took years to burst on the scene—more than thirty years, in fact. Though one in three U.S. homes now boasts at least one Scrabble set, when first conceived by Alfred Mosher Butts, an architect out of work during the Depression, the game didn't have a one-in-a-million chance.

With time on his hands, Butts decided to create a board game. And he was going to do it right. He analyzed the market and concluded there were three types of games that were successful—number games (bingo), strategy or move games (checkers, chess) and word games (anagrams). He combined the three in a game he first called Lexico (1931) and later renamed Criss Cross Words.

But what about that letter distribution? (And how come we never get an "S" when we need one?) Butts studied the front page of the *New York Times* and calculated how frequently each letter was used. The more frequent the letter, the lower the point value. Ingenious, certainly. But still no one wanted to buy the game until Butts met James Brunot.

A fellow entrepreneur, Brunot liked Butts's game and together they refined the rules and dubbed it Scrabble, meaning "to grope frantically after the action of drawing letter tiles." The game was trademarked and launched in 1948, but it didn't move.

So how did Scrabble go from zip in 1948 to selling two million sets by the end of the twentieth century? The popular story goes that in 1952 the president of Macy's discovered the game while on vacation and ordered some for the store. A year later, it was the game that everyone had to have. Butts lived to see his game become a phenomenon and watched it go through a variety of manufacturers, from Selchow & Righter to Milton Bradley today. It's said Butts loved playing his game right up until his death at age 93 in 1993.

National Champion Joel Sherman's winning board in the National Scrabble Association's National Scrabble Championship, San Diego, California, August 2002

TRIPLE WORD SCORE   DOUBLE LETTER SCORE   TRIPLE WORD SCORE   DOUBLE LETTER SCORE   W$_4$ A$_1$ X$_8$

D$_2$ TRIPLE LETTER SCORE   V$_4$ I$_1$ P$_3$ E$_1$ R$_1$

T$_1$ E$_1$ N$_1$ U$_1$ R$_1$ E$_1$ DOUBLE LETTER SCORE   I$_1$ N$_1$ DOUBLE WORD SCORE

DOUBLE LETTER SCORE   N$_1$ H$_4$ E$_1$ L$_1$ I$_1$ C$_3$ O$_1$ I$_1$ D$_2$ S$_1$ DOUBLE LETTER SCORE

I$_1$ DOUBLE WORD SCORE   N$_1$ O$_1$ O$_1$

M$_3$ TRIPLE LETTER SCORE   A$_1$ L$_1$ P$_3$ TRIPLE LETTER SCORE

DOUBLE LETTER SCORE   DOUBLE LETTER SCORE   DOUBLE LETTER SCORE   R$_1$ E$_1$ DOUBLE LETTER SCORE

TRIPLE WORD SCORE   DOUBLE LETTER SCORE   Q$_{10}$ A$_1$ DOUBLE LETTER SCORE   O$_1$ A$_1$ K$_5$

DOUBLE LETTER SCORE   O$_1$ U$_1$ T$_1$ B$_3$ O$_1$ E$_1$ D$_2$

J$_8$ V$_4$ A$_1$ L$_1$ Z$_{10}$

B$_3$ O$_1$ M$_3$ U$_1$ I$_1$ E$_1$ F$_4$ E$_1$ T$_1$

Y$_4$ F$_4$ R$_1$ U$_1$ G$_2$ A$_1$ L$_1$ R$_1$ DOUBLE WORD SCORE   H$_4$

T$_1$ W$_4$ A$_1$ DOUBLE LETTER SCORE   DOUBLE LETTER SCORE   R$_1$ A$_1$ G$_2$ DOUBLE WORD SCORE   E$_1$

E$_1$ DOUBLE WORD SCORE   G$_2$ A$_1$ D$_2$ I$_1$ I$_1$ TRIPLE LETTER SCORE   N$_1$ DOUBLE WORD SCORE   I$_1$

S$_1$ Y$_4$ E$_1$ T$_1$ I$_1$ S$_1$ C$_3$ DOUBLE LETTER SCORE   N$_1$

Copyright 1948 by SELCHOW & RIGHTER CO., Printed in U.S.A.

The scale of one inch
to one foot has been
the standard for real-
istic dollhouses since
the 1930s.

F. W BRIGGS

c. 1930 Dollhouse

Throughout the first years of the twentieth century, many toys for older children centered on role-play. To be sure, there were games and sporting equipment, but one of the functions of play was to help children prepare for their roles in the world, and during these years those roles were often defined by gender. For girls, though not universally, that meant being a homemaker and mother.

Dolls were designed to teach nurturing and caretaking. There were all kinds of play tools related to cooking and cleaning, and miniature versions of everything from mangles to mops were designed to allow girls to feel grown up—and just like their mothers and grandmothers.

"Playing house" was what it was all about, and during this period many beautiful dollhouses allowed little girls' imaginations to create and manage a world in miniature in which they were solely in control and felt very grown-up.

The vast majority of dollhouses were made by individuals, very often as replicas of real houses, but they could also be simpler affairs. Dollhouse furniture was commercially available through a wide number of manufacturers—including Ideal, Schoenhut, Tootsietoy and many more. The standard scale was one inch to one foot, which remained unchanged throughout the rest of the century.

In the post–World War II years, plastics began being used in dollhouses, and in the 1950s and 1960s, manufacturers made metal doll-houses, which were hugely popular.

While little girls in the twenty-first century have many more opportunities available to them, playing house has never gone out of style, and millions continue to create magical, imaginary worlds with their dolls and dollhouses.

The Briggs Dollhouse, c. 1930, created by Fordham Briggs, is a rare example of the traditional handcrafted dollhouses that were used for both play and display, and an accurate representation—in miniature—of the style and decorating modes of its time

This exterior opened up to reveal the rooms on the opposite page

1933

After the crash in 1929, America seemed to lose heart. In the face of rising unemployment, scarce and low-paying work and general disillusionment, the excesses and exuberance of the 1920s seemed, well, silly. Income had dropped by as much as forty percent and, as the Dust Bowl further hobbled the country, people looked for hope anywhere they could find it. ■ Still, though struggling, they didn't give up, and popular culture thrived in its way. With all the economic challenges, the role of government was paramount. Social Security was established in 1935. Programs like the

Midtown Manhattan, c. 1938

WPA put skilled artisans to work, and landmarks such as the Empire State Building and Rockefeller Center went up during this period, tributes to humans' unquenchable spirit. ■ Entertainment was largely focused on the home, with parlor games and board games becoming hugely popular, helping people believe that better times were ahead. Monopoly let people at least dream of being millionaires, and a renewed nationwide focus on the importance of

1933-1942 Depression and the Road to War

education inspired Milton Bradley's 1938 hit, Go to the Head of the Class, reinforcing the idea that smarts would make America great again and help win the war on the Depression and the war overseas. Mickey Mouse continued to win hearts on-screen and in products. Yet no one toy before or since would create the kind of excitement that the Shirley Temple doll did. ■ Radio was free, and this was its golden age, as eighty percent of U.S. homes tuned in to Fred Allen, George

Burns and Gracie Allen, Jack Benny, Fibber McGee and Molly and Will Rogers. Perhaps the most famous radio broadcast of the decade, though, was Orson Welles's performance of "The War of the Worlds," which convinced the audience that Martians were actually invading Earth. ■ People danced to the big-band sounds of Tommy Dorsey, Benny Goodman and Glenn Miller and swung with Duke Ellington. In sports, Joe Louis defeated Max Schmeling in a bout that

became associated with America's ability to trounce

Germany, and professional sports continued to attract passionate fans. Horse racing became legal, and there was a boom in winter sports, driven in large measure by the 1932 Winter Olympics and stars like skater Sonja Henie, who would later be immortalized as a doll

Shirley Temple, c. 1930s

New York Yankees baseball players Lou Gehrig and Babe Ruth, c. 1930

Marlene Dietrich, *Blond Venus*, 1942

by Madame Alexander. ("When she saw how beautiful I made her nose, she had hers fixed to match," Madame said in an interview near the end of her life.) ■ Escape from the cares of the world at the movies cost a nickel. Hollywood produced hilarious escapist tales and stories of romance that gave people something to cling to. Fred and Ginger encouraged folks to tap their troubles away. Greta Garbo, Joan Crawford and Marlene Dietrich were idolized and presented women with models of self-reliance and independence—important qualities for a troubled nation. But no movie star would capture the hearts of the nation more than Shirley Temple. Her resolute cheeriness even in the face of disaster was an amazingly powerful tonic. To twenty-first century eyes, her movies may seem overly precious, but in the mid-1930s her performances were just the ticket. A tap-dancing beacon of hope, Shirley ruled the box office and created a huge market for merchandise, especially the dolls mentioned earlier. Toward the end of the decade, *Gone with the Wind* would debut, and Walt Disney would pioneer the full-length animated movie with *Snow White and the Seven Dwarfs* in 1937, followed by *Fantasia* (1940), *Dumbo* (1941) and *Bambi* (1942). ■ Americans also got a glimpse of the future at the New York World's Fair in 1939. Themed "Building the World of Tomorrow," the fair challenged people to think ahead to the distant world of 1960 in an exhibition called

Sonja Henie, c. 1940

"Futurama," in which television, multi-lane highways (with possible speeds of 100 miles per hour) and new housing developments were shown dominating the culture. Under the iconic Trylon and Perisphere construction, the fair was designed to be a showcase for the visionary thinking and design that would shape the years to come. ■ As the decade progressed, for all the growing optimism at home, instability and chaos ruled overseas. Hitler rose to power, conquering Europe virtually unchecked, except for a struggling Great Britain. Japan pushed toward war, and

Trylon and Perisphere, New York World's Fair, 1939

the U.S. responded with isolationism, at least until December 7, 1941, when Japan's attack on Pearl Harbor brought the U.S. into the war. Immediately, the nation mobilized with countless programs designed to support the war effort. The country went back to work with a common goal and a vision of the future that the U.S. would risk all to protect.

1934 Shirley Temple Doll

Some say Shirley Temple brought America out of the Great Depression with her resolute good cheer and sunshiny disposition. (Cranky, less toy-loving people will likely point to the New Deal, changes in monetary policy and the approach of World War II as the major causes for the end of the Depression.) However, no one can question the little star's box-office clout. She literally saved Fox Studios from bankruptcy and became one of the biggest box-office draws of all time.

Certainly from a product perspective, Shirley Temple created a kind of craze that was never equaled throughout the rest of the century. When Ideal Novelty & Toy Company launched its first Shirley Temple Doll in 1934, it was an instant phenomenon, with people standing in line for days in hopes of buying one. The country was just starting the long process of emerging from the Depression, people were beginning to spend money and it wasn't just Shirley Temple Dolls they wanted, but underwear, soap, hats, overcoats, sheet music and virtually anything that featured the star's likeness or endorsement. Later toy fads pale by comparison, as never before and never since has virtually an entire country so loved one little girl.

Ideal held the exclusive license to manufacture the dolls, and the original composition dolls were made from 1934 to 1939 in a variety of costumes from Shirley Temple's movies. The dolls were consistent best-sellers and became the most successful celebrity dolls in history. In 1957, Ideal released vinyl Shirley Temple dolls in different sizes to coincide with the release of Shirley Temple's movies on television. The company produced dolls again in the '70s and '80s.

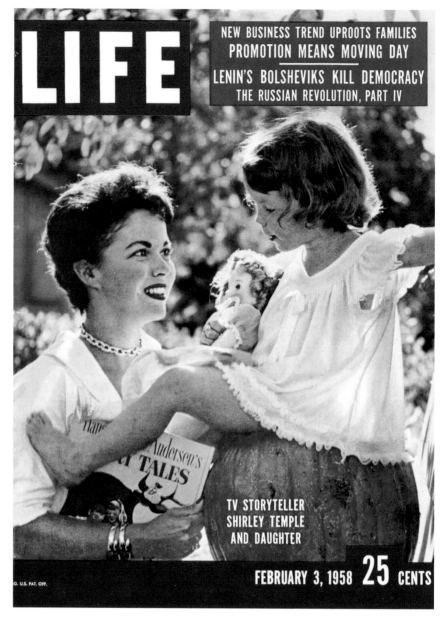

Three generations—Shirley Temple Black, her daughter Susan, and the timeless doll

Shirley Temple Black herself solved one of the mysteries surrounding the dolls in the early 1980s. Although the 1930s dolls were phenomenally popular, they never really quite looked like Shirley Temple. But at one point the sculpting changed and the dolls seemed more accurately to represent the young Shirley. Black said the change happened when she took over the approval of her image from her mother. As with most mothers, Shirley's had always had an idealized view of her daughter and wanted that image for the dolls. Shirley Temple Black herself was somewhat more realistic.

Nonetheless, Shirley Temple dolls remain among the most prized collectibles.

1935
Monopoly

Parker Brothers originally rejected Monopoly, citing fifty-two "design flaws." The company never said what, exactly, they were.

What fantasy was more compelling during the Depression than the idea of living on "Easy Street"? While the reality was out of reach for millions of people who were barely getting by, they could dream of cornering the real estate market in Atlantic City, and when Monopoly was introduced by Charles B. Darrow in 1935, the public—eager for an hour or two of wheeling, dealing and escape from the everyday—made it an instant hit.

But it was a hit that almost didn't happen. Darrow had shown the game to Parker Brothers in 1934, but due to its fifty-two "design flaws" (to this day still unknown) it was rejected. Out of work like many Americans at the time, Darrow and a printer friend created five thousand copies and convinced a Philadelphia department store to sell the game, where it became a swift sellout.

With a clear success on his hands and unable to keep up with demand, Darrow went back to Parker Brothers, who this time somehow managed to overlook the design errors. The game became an instant hit—and has never been out of production since.

Monopoly became so much a part of the U.S. culture that it even was used as a tool of espionage in World War II. Seemingly innocent copies of the game were sent to American prisoners in German POW camps, with maps and other information in the board—and real money inserted into the packs of play money. Though not quite a "Get Out of Jail Free" card, it was a huge help as prisoners escaped.

Today, Monopoly is played in eighty countries and produced in twenty-six languages and a wide variety of special-interest versions. One would guess the dream of a hotel on Boardwalk is something to which everyone everywhere can always relate.

Flaws notwithstanding, Darrow and a printer friend created five thousand copies of the game and sold them in a local department store.

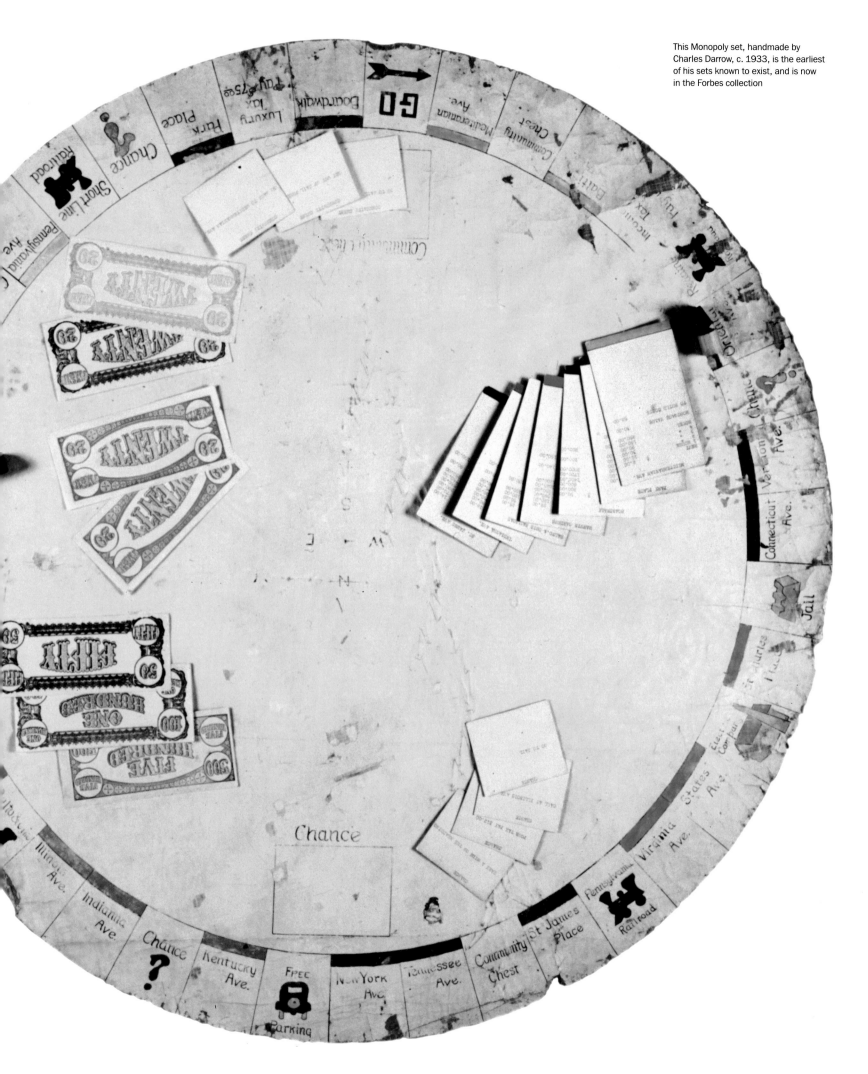

This Monopoly set, handmade by Charles Darrow, c. 1933, is the earliest of his sets known to exist, and is now in the Forbes collection

1938 Snoopy
Sniffer

Snoopy Sniffer hit the beach in the 1938 Miss America Pageant, where he was photographed as much as the contestants.

This adorable wooden pull-toy with the floppy ears and oilcloth feet was to become one of the best-selling toys of all time, selling more than ten million units over forty-three years. Yet when he was first introduced in 1938, it was anyone's guess whether the toy would be successful or the company would even survive.

Fisher-Price had first shown its toys at the 1932 Toy Fair trade show in New York, a year after the company was founded by Herman G. Fischer, Irving Price and Helen M. Schelle. But like many new companies in the Depression, the going wasn't always easy.

At the time, pull-toys were staples of the toy chest, and the Snoopy Sniffer was designed to look and sound like a real dog. Finally, Fisher-Price had a hit toy, and Snoopy would do more than entertain children--he would make Fisher-Price profitable for the first time.

In fact, Snoopy Sniffer became so popular that it was issued its own State of New York Dog Tag, making it a real dog, at least in the eyes of East Aurora, New York, where in 1954, tag number 278471 was issued. Snoopy's age was listed as 17--"Quite old for a dog," the town clerk is said to have quipped.

In his early years, Snoopy Sniffer also hit the beach with the contestants in the 1938 Miss America Pageant, where he was photographed almost as much as the beautiful girls. Forty-three years later, now a childhood classic, Snoopy Sniffer would take a walk down the Champs-Elysees with Henry Kors, then president of Fisher-Price.

Snoopy Sniffer was produced through 1981, halting only during the years of World War II when the Fisher-Price factories were turned over to the manufacture of goods needed for the war effort. Over the years, Snoopy Sniffer was produced in four different sizes and looks, becoming a true classic. Always dependable and ready to play, he was for many children their first "real" dog.

1940
View-Master

View-Master through the decades: The original, c. 1940, and the sixtieth Anniversary edition in 2000

Although he lacked the capital to start his own business, Gruber was out photographing deer one day with his 3-D equipment when he met Harold Graves, president of a photography company. Together the men formed a partnership that resulted in the mass-market production of the View-Master. Unveiled at the New York and San Francisco world's fairs in 1940, it was an instant hit, and a year later it was being sold by some thousand retailers.

During World War II, film, plastic and paper shortages almost put the company out of business. But the Army and Navy realized the product had immense training potential, and ordered 100,000 viewers and six million reels. The government literally saved this toy, which has remained a classic, as generations of children continue to be enthralled by the magic their eyes perceive.

The concept of stereo vision has fascinated people since the ancient Greek mathematician Euclid first identified and demonstrated binocular vision. But it wasn't until the advent of photography in the nineteenth century that people were able to experience three-dimensional visuals on a mass scale. In the 1850s, the stereopticon became a sensation on both sides of the Atlantic, and viewing 3-D pictures of exotic locations was considered exciting home entertainment.

Nearly a century later, William Gruber came up with the idea of using color movie film in a handheld viewing device with two eyepieces. Two photos taken from slightly different perspectives and overlaid on one another created the effect. Gruber went the stereopticon one better—using film instead of photos on cards and putting ten different images on a reel that fit into his viewer.

View-Master, c. 1950

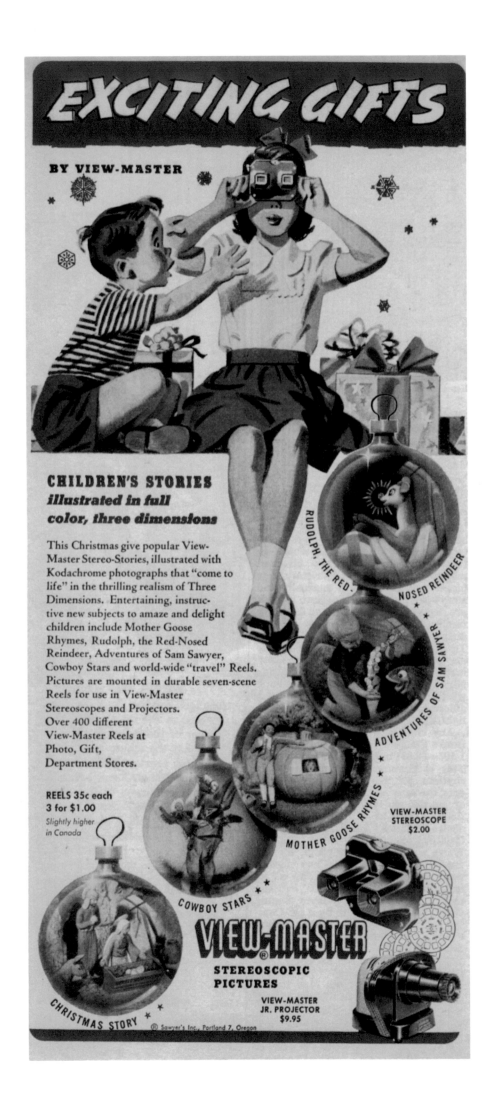

The war dominated everything—music, art, literature, sports. Everything that could be used to contribute to the war effort was. There was rationing of food and the Victory Garden—popularized during WWI—became a staple again, providing as much as forty percent of the produce consumed in the U.S. during the period. Women went to work in huge numbers for the first time. Even teenagers went to work and experienced adult responsibility and income. Unemployment, which had been rampant in the years leading up to the war, was eliminated, as every able-bodied worker did what he or she could to contribute. ■ Due to metal rationing, automobile production was stopped in 1942, as was manufacturing of anything nonessential for domestic life. Virtually all factories in the nation were dedicated to producing materials for the war effort, including toy factories such as those owned by Hedstrom, Buddy L, Radio Flyer and Fisher-Price. Some toys that had been made out of metal, such as Buddy L trucks, were made from wood during these years. ■ A huge part of the war effort was devoted to the development of products and technologies that, when applied to peacetime industries, would transform product design, manufac-

Betty Grable, 1943

1943-1952
War and
Recovery

ture and consumption. Penicillin helped battlefield injuries and would transform medicine back home. New plastics would show up in toys, appliances and much more. Advanced metal fabrication techniques would help make the home swing set popular. And the first computers would begin to revolutionize business. Food storage techniques, particularly those developed by Birdseye, would make convenience foods available to women who had spent the war years working, and as television began to spread around the nation, the TV dinner would become a fixture in many homes. ■ In entertainment, radio still dominated at the beginning of the decade, but by 1951, more than fifteen million television sets would be installed in homes, and classic radio shows would make their way to TV. While Milton Berle and Ed Sullivan entertained adults, the first generation of kids to grow up with television was enthralled by Kukla Fran and Ollie and "The Howdy Doody Show." Westerns, which had been hugely popular in the movies, giddyapped to TV with such stars as Roy Rogers kids' capturing attention. In 1951, "Pioneer Playhouse" would be one of the first shows to inspire kids' play—and sell toys. ■ There wasn't much time for play during

Kaye Popp and Stanley Catron dancing the lindy hop, 1943

U.S. metal-toy factory, 1946

"Buffalo" Bob Smith with Howdy Doody, from the television series, "The Howdy Doody Show," c. 1948

the war—at least not for older folks—and rationing made materials for new toys scarce. One of the by-products of the war effort—a spring—became a quintessential toy of the period, ultimately known as Slinky. Toward the end of this decade, the Western craze had captivated both boys and girls, though earlier games remained popular and were establishing themselves as classics. Wooden model sets from companies like Strombecker and Carrom Games' Nok-Hockey were hits, and after the war metal, plastic and electricity combined in one of the most popular boys' games of the next decades—Tudor Metal's Tru Action Electric Football. No, it wasn't as realistic as the games that would follow, but for the time it was magical. ■ For older folks, dancing and nightclubbing were primary entertainments. People did the jitterbug and the lindy hop to the sounds of the big bands, and stompin' at the Savoy was a major Saturday night event. ■ Movies celebrated homespun values and American virtues.

Marilyn Monroe, *The Seven-Year Itch*, 1955

Classics like *Mrs. Miniver, The Best Years of Our Lives, Lifeboat, Casablanca* and many others were part of

Buddy L wooden truck, c. 1945

what the Office of War believed was essential communication to keep people's feelings of confidence and patriotism at a fever pitch. Escapist fare propelled the popular screwball comedies, and movie stars were idolized as never before. ■ The privations of the war also influenced fashion. Newly working women wore utilitarian clothing that could go from the workplace to a night out, and pants became acceptable on women, a look featured in many movies of the time, particularly those starring Katharine Hepburn. When stockings were scarce (both nylon and silk were essential to the war), women used eyebrow pencil to draw simulated seams on the backs of their legs. At the end of the war, fuller silhouettes returned and the look was very feminine. ■ And once home, the returning GIs and their newly growing families drove an economic recovery that was unprecedented as they bought homes and settled into peacetime. America had proven its might, and it was time to enjoy all the advantages the country offered.

Glenn Miller, 1944

"What walks down stairs, alone or in pairs, and makes a slinkity sound? A spring, a spring, a marvelous thing. Everyone knows it's Slinky..."

Any kid who was watching TV during the 1960s, could easily sing along with the above jingle from the now-classic TV commercial. But the real story of Slinky began nearly twenty years earlier, when engineer Richard James was working on suspension systems on a ship during World War II. One day, James watched a large torsion spring fall to the deck and begin to do what would become known as the "Slinky Walk." Fascinated, and thinking that perhaps there was a toy idea here, James took the spring home.

His wife, Betty, agreed that simple as it was, the walking spring was fun. It was she who named the toy, after rummaging through a dictionary for just the right word. Hitting on "slinky" as a word that described the toy's movement, Richard and Betty set out to develop and manufacture it. With trial, error and a bit of luck (three essential components of toy development), they fashioned the final toy out of more than eighty feet of wire perfectly coiled to give it just the right weight and movement.

They formed James Industries and began selling the toy at Gimbel's in Philadelphia for the 1945 holiday season, and sales were tremendous. In the 1950s, suddenly single and with a family to raise, Betty took the reins of the company and just kept innovating—introducing all kinds of new Slinkys. From animals to plastic to gold-plate, Slinky always seemed "now" and marvelous to kids. The Slinky Dog was later immortalized in the movie *Toy Story*, and at almost sixty years old, nearly 275 million Slinkys made of fifty thousand tons of wire have been sold. And they've used enough wire to encircle the globe 126 times.

Over the years, Betty James became one of the most beloved and respected figures in the toy industry. She was inducted into the Toy Industry Hall of Fame in 2000. Yet to talk to many women in the toy industry today, perhaps one of her most important achievements was that she always had time to talk, to share ideas and inspire women to be entrepreneurs, to follow their dreams and create success for themselves.

1945 Slinky

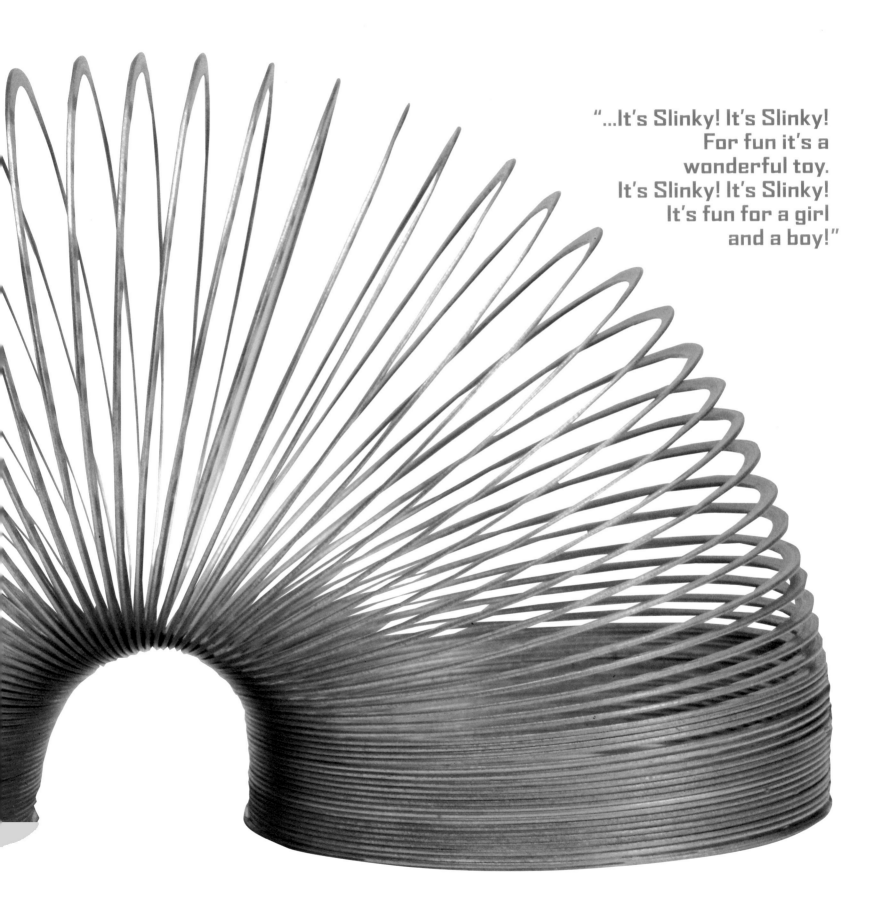

"...It's Slinky! It's Slinky!
For fun it's a
wonderful toy.
It's Slinky! It's Slinky!
It's fun for a girl
and a boy!"

1947
Wonder Spring
Horse

The rocking horse
galloped into the
twentieth century
with suspended
springs, for a more
"realistic" ride.

What could be more exciting for the young cowboy or cowgirl than saddling up a favorite horse and galloping across the plains? Of course, in post–World War II America, though the desire was strong, and Westerns ruled kids' imaginative play, the wide open plains were a little far from the suburban homestead, to say nothing of zoning and the problems of horse ownership in a subdivision. Besides, it was kind of tough to light out for the territory and be home in time for dinner, homework and bed.

Well, the next best thing, as is always the case, would be to imagine. In 1947, the Wonder Products company introduced the first spring horse—the ideal way for kids to feel no one could fence them in...without ever leaving the family room.

The spring horse was a cutout wooden horse suspended within a frame by four very sturdy springs. It was, essentially, a new take on the rocking horse that had been a childhood classic for centuries. What the springs added was the ability to simulate the real gait of a horse better than ever before.

The Wonder Horse, as it came to be called, was a hit, and it would be manufactured through the mid-1980s. Over that time the body, which continued to be decorated with freehand airbrush painting, would change to plastic, and even as manufacturing was increasingly moving offshore, the plants in Bossier City would continue to turn out the huge rotational plastic molds that could make a full horse body in one shot.

Wonder would continue to innovate throughout its history, creating the first motion-activated sound horse, Clip-Clop, and a stable full of other horses. In the late 1980s, Wonder rode off into the sunset, but many of the company's innovations are still used in contemporary spring horses.

c. 1947
Doctor and Nurse Kits

There was something pretty amazing about doctors—they held, or seemed to hold, the answer to the mysteries of our bodies, something kids are naturally fascinated with as they grow up.

In the years following WWII, it seemed like there were medical miracles happening all the time. Diseases were cured and vaccines developed, and that was only the beginning of what would happen over the next decades. The enduring scourges of childhood—polio, measles, mumps and more—would fall to the triumphant advances of science.

Doctors and nurses were heroes well respected within their communities, and going to the doctor for checkups and treatment was a regular activity for kids. They worked magic: If you were sick, they made you well. Where did that amazing power come from?

Given that these were amazing human beings to kids, it was only natural that doctoring would translate into children's play. There was also something pretty cool about doctors—they held, or seemed to hold, the answer to the mysteries of our bodies, something kids are naturally fascinated with as they grow up. Who growing up at the time didn't at some point want to be one of these trusted, slightly mysterious and oh-so-knowledgeable professionals?

Pressman Toy Corporation, as well as many other companies, realized that doctor role-playing was very popular. And they responded with kits that included everything from stethoscopes to hypodermics to "real rubber gloves," tongue depressors and all the equipment a make-believe doctor needs.

Though they enjoyed their greatest sales in the '50s and early '60s, driven by popular characters such as Dr. Kildare, Ben Casey and later Marcus Welby and even the team on "M.A.S.H." doctor and nurse kits remain among the classic role-playing toys. But what has made this type of play so appealing over time is that as they grow, little children are fascinated by their bodies, so it's only natural that they would want to imagine that they could work the same kind of magic that doctors can.

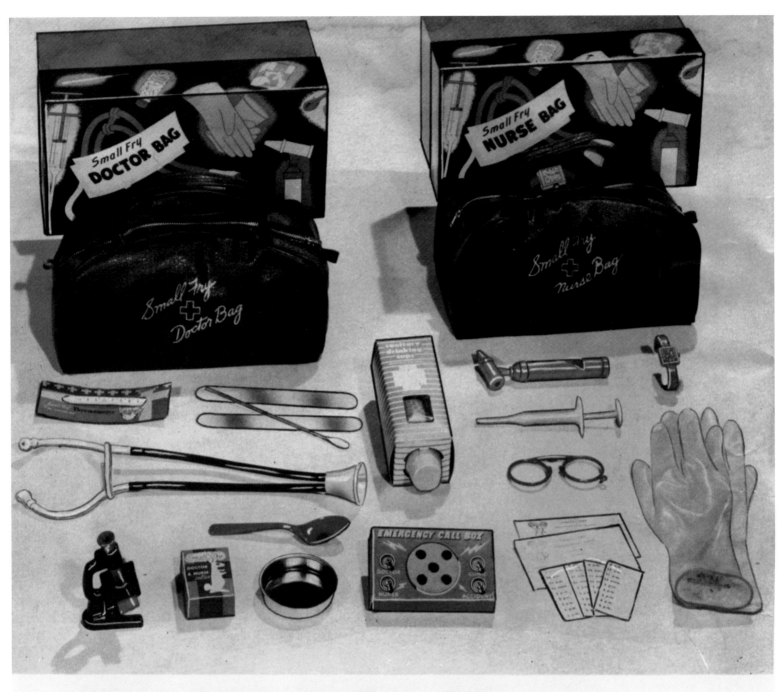

"Super" Doctor and Nurse Bags

Featuring the EXCITING, NEW, "Emergency Call Box"

All new colorful plastic parts in the "just like real" leatherette zippered bag.

Each Doctor and Nurse Bag Contains:

Emergency Call Box	Plastic Watch	Applicator	Plastic Hypo Needle
White Enameled Thermometer	Plastic Stethescope	Appointment Slips	Cup Dispenser with 6 cups
Plastic Eyeglasses	Prescription Sheets	Tongue Depressors	Plastic Eye and Ear Detector

EXTRA! Each Doctor Bag contains a real microscope, each Nurse Bag contains rubber gloves.

No. 3394 DOCTOR BAG

1 DOZEN TO CARTON   WEIGHT 18 LBS.

No. 3396 NURSE BAG

1 DOZEN TO CARTON   WEIGHT 17 LBS.

Everybody Loves Pressman Toys

It seems as if every civilization and every time has had favorite ways of telling the future. In fifteenth-century Italy, tarot cards made their first appearance, and in the Victorian age, seers marketed crude gizmos and gadgets designed to help the beclouded commune with the spirit world and determine their destinies. In 1892, in the United States, this future fascination went mass-market with the introduction of the Ouija board. Consumers couldn't get enough.

In the late 1940s, Alabe Crafts introduced the Magic 8 Ball, ostensibly because to be "behind the 8 ball" is to be in a pickle, and this shake-and-see answer-giver would help you make the right choices, though it was marketed "for entertainment purposes only."

Like any good fortune-telling device, the Magic 8 Ball is simple to operate. Ask it a question. Give it a shake. And wait. In a few moments the answer floats into the window on the bottom—also known as "the Spirit Slate." The Magic 8 Ball's answers are always noncommittal and, like those of any fortune-teller worthy of a palm crossed with silver, open to interpretation. So whether it's "Signs Point to Yes," "Outlook Not So Good," "My Reply is No" or "Better Not Tell You Now," sadly the Magic 8 Ball can only point the way. No matter, we'll keep looking for answers and relying on this classic kitsch icon.

And you can bet that whatever the answer—particularly if it's "Reply Hazy Try Again"—people will keep trying for many generations to come.

1947 Magic 8 Ball

"For entertainment purposes only..."

1947
Nok-Hockey

Developed for the kids of New York, Nok-Hockey brought a popular street game indoors.

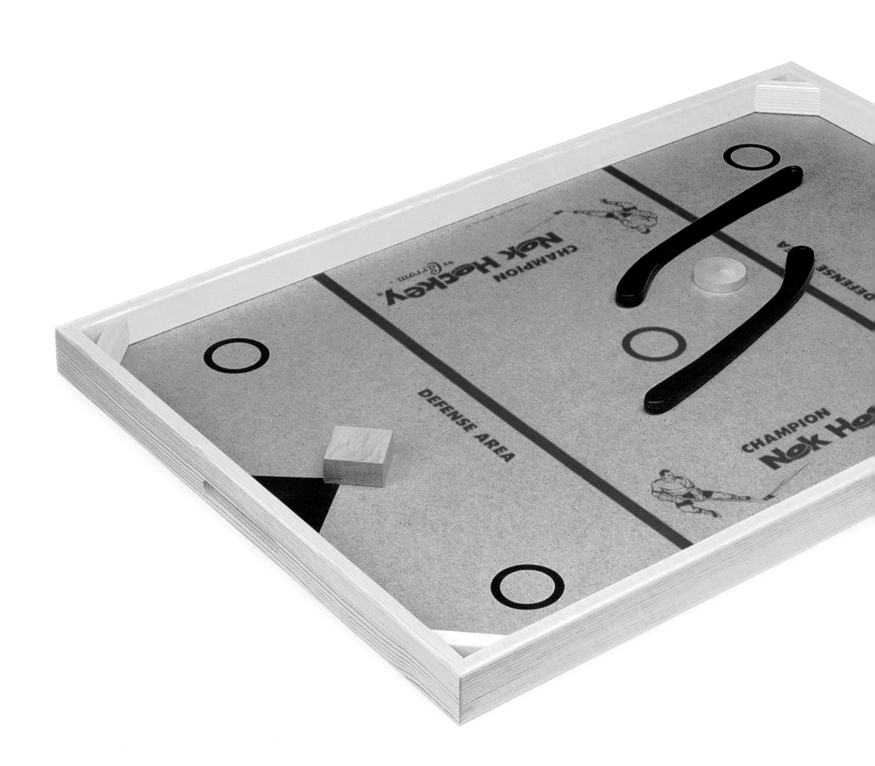

Carrom's Nok-Hockey was first introduced in 1947 as a way for kids to take the popular sport of street hockey indoors. Along with stoop ball, stick ball and the "Spaldeen big pinkie," it became a classic, competitive game that's never been out of production since it was introduced.

Part of the appeal of Nok-Hockey, even to twenty-first century players, is how simple it is—made of nothing more than a pine board with wooden blocks to protect the goal and a screened playing surface. The object is to hit your puck into your opponent's goal. It's all about controlled mayhem. Oh, and noise. This is a game that is characterized by the clattering of the puck as it is slapped around the playing area. And if the puck flies off the surface, just drop it back in and play continues. As in all the classic street games, kids always reveled in making up their own house rules, and it was as much about the excitement of play as it was about winning. Of course, whether or not one was winning could be a matter of debate. Even the printed rules that came with the game put that decision in the hands of the players; it's the action that counts.

Nok-Hockey would inspire other action games and classic wooden parlor games. It was the forefather of air hockey, which would be a huge hit from the 1970s onward. Yet Nok-Hockey's simple, sturdy structure and open-ended competition means that it will always have a special place on the game shelf.

1948
Cootie

Cootie was such a beloved game that it became a tradition for many years in the Macy's Thanksgiving Day parade

In 1948, Herb Schaper created the Cootie game, one of the forerunners of the so-called skill-and-action games that were hugely popular in the '60s and beyond. In these games, there was no traditional board. Rather, players used game pieces to create the game. In the case of Cootie, those pieces were parts of a bug, and the game was a race to be the first to assemble the bug, with rolls of the die telling you which piece to put in when. In some families, it was the practice for the winner to jump around as though actually having Cooties—in what was called the "Cootie Dance."

Cootie became a huge hit and a real rage among preschoolers in the early '50s, and it has stayed popular ever since, particularly because the game is inherently silly, the bugs are cute and the game lends itself to the creation of "family rules," as with the Cootie Dance mentioned above.

The first sets were all made by hand in wood by the folks at Schaper before they turned to mass production. Nearly half a million sets are said to have been made by hand. The Cootie was so popular that it became a balloon in Macy's Thanksgiving Day parade, and it's still manufactured by Milton Bradley.

In some families, it was the practice for the winner to jump around as though actually having Cooties—in what was called the "Cootie Dance."

1949
Candy Land

"A sweet little game...
for sweet little folks."

How many millions of kids have first learned about the luck of the draw, fair play and the excitement of board games from Candy Land? With millions and millions sold since its debut in 1949, the game has clearly become a part of American culture and a treasured memory from childhood.

While not intended as a learning game originally, Candy Land wrapped the learning of basic counting and color skills in a magical world where the Peppermint Stick Forest, Fudge Swamp, Gumdrop Mountain and much more provided irresistible temptation and fun for the youngest game players.

The game was developed by Eleanor Abbott, who was recovering from childhood polio and astutely realized that a game about favorite treats would have a lot more appeal than one about, say, vegetables. She probably didn't have any idea that her "sweet little game for sweet little folks" would virtually create the preschool game category and become an all-time classic.

Since it first came out, Candy Land has never been out of production. Three generations have shared this delightful game, and when asked what games they remember playing as children, adults always put Candy Land on the list. In addition to its original version, Candy Land has gone high-tech with electronic handheld and CD-ROM versions. In 2002, Milton Bradley created a special version of the game exclusively for Walt Disney World—uniting two of the sweetest childhood experiences of all time.

A game about favorite treats has a lot more appeal than one about, say, vegetables.

1949 Clue

How do you while away the time when your city is under siege and you're in a blackout? During the Second World War, many Londoners trapped inside during the blitz invented parlor games, one of which was called Murder. The game, which also featured in detective fiction, was a kind of tag and deduction game with the frisson of fear enhanced by the fact that it had to be played in the dark.

Law clerk Anthony E. Pratt designed his version of the game in 1943, but it wasn't until three years later that it went into production. A year later, Parker Brothers licensed it and introduced it first in Australia and later in the U.S. Now called Cluedo in the U.K. and Clue elsewhere, the game became a huge hit, in part due to the fascination with crime inspired by Agatha Christie and the classic murder mystery films of Alfred Hitchcock that were made throughout the early 1950s.

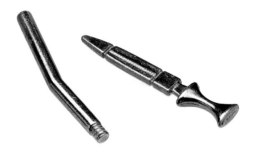

Clue has always been a relatively simple game. Players select a murderer from among the characters, a murder weapon and a room in which the dastardly crime took place. The challenge is to unravel the mystery by moving from room to room and asking questions.

Today, the game is still one of the top-ten selling games, and there have been a variety of versions introduced for children, using licensed characters. In 2002, Parker Brothers unveiled a special edition at Walt Disney World themed to its Haunted Mansion attraction.

There has always been something inherently intriguing and entertaining about solving mysteries—and beating your opponents to the solution. One might even say that the appeal of such a game is...elementary.

1950
Red Trike

A child's first set of wheels, the trike became ubiquitous in the expanding postwar suburbs.

For children in the postwar era, the classic Red Trike from Hedstrom was a primary means of transportation. During World War II, Hedstrom had turned to producing essentials for the war effort. But with peacetime came a new heyday for children's products for the young baby boomers and their families. For Hedstrom, that meant a resurgence in production of, and demand for, the Red Trike, first introduced in the 1930s. Originally called a "velocipede" and based on the three-wheeled conveyances of the nineteenth century, the Trike was streamlined and scaled down for children.

For adventures at the end of the driveway or excursions down the sidewalk, there was simply nothing better. An entire generation of kids grew up in the then-expanding suburbs, and many recall spending full days pedaling and playing, for in the imagination, a tricycle could become anything from a race car to a space exploration vehicle. The point was, there was mobility, and the child was in control.

The Red Trike became a classic, known for its sturdy construction that never needed servicing or repair. The black tires on white rims were made of virtually indestructible nylon. The frame was bright red, and the pedals were single blocks of rubber. Adults who grew up riding this trike remember the pride they took in it and the freedom it gave them.

The memories created by one's first set of wheels are often indelible, and for millions of kids from the 1930s through today, the Hedstrom Red Trike is recalled with affection, excitement and fondness for that first taste of freewheeling freedom.

WHEEL TOYS · 1950

by *Hedstrom*

Even the biggest stars started out in small parts. Of course, in the case of Fisher-Price's Little People, they started out *as* small parts.

In 1950, Fisher-Price created the Looky Fire Truck, manned by three roundheaded, wooden abstract firemen that were permanently attached to the toy. Over the rest of the decade, these bit players gave wooden but imaginative performances in a stagecoach, robot and sports car, each time in increasingly bigger parts. In other words, they would move when the toys were pushed along the floor.

It was 1959 when the characters burst from obscurity in the Safety School Bus—and five of the formerly stationary characters became separate toys. Adults who remember the toys from that period recall playing with the chunky wooden peg people and the fun of pretending to go to school. Throughout the '60s, the peg characters began to appear in all kinds of classic play sets—trains, farms, amusement parks, a dump truck—and became so popular that they began to be sold separately under the name Play Family.

In 1975, the first license was introduced to the line: The peg people found sunny days on "Sesame Street." Ten years later, the Play Family was renamed Little People, though they still retained their peg-like look.

In 1997, the characters finally became more people-like with arms, legs and dimensional faces, and in 1999, Fisher-Price reintroduced the Little People School Bus—a fortieth-anniversary version of the toy that started it all.

No matter what they've looked like, however, for more than forty years, the Little People have had one thing in common—they always made the child and the child's imagination the star of the playtime show.

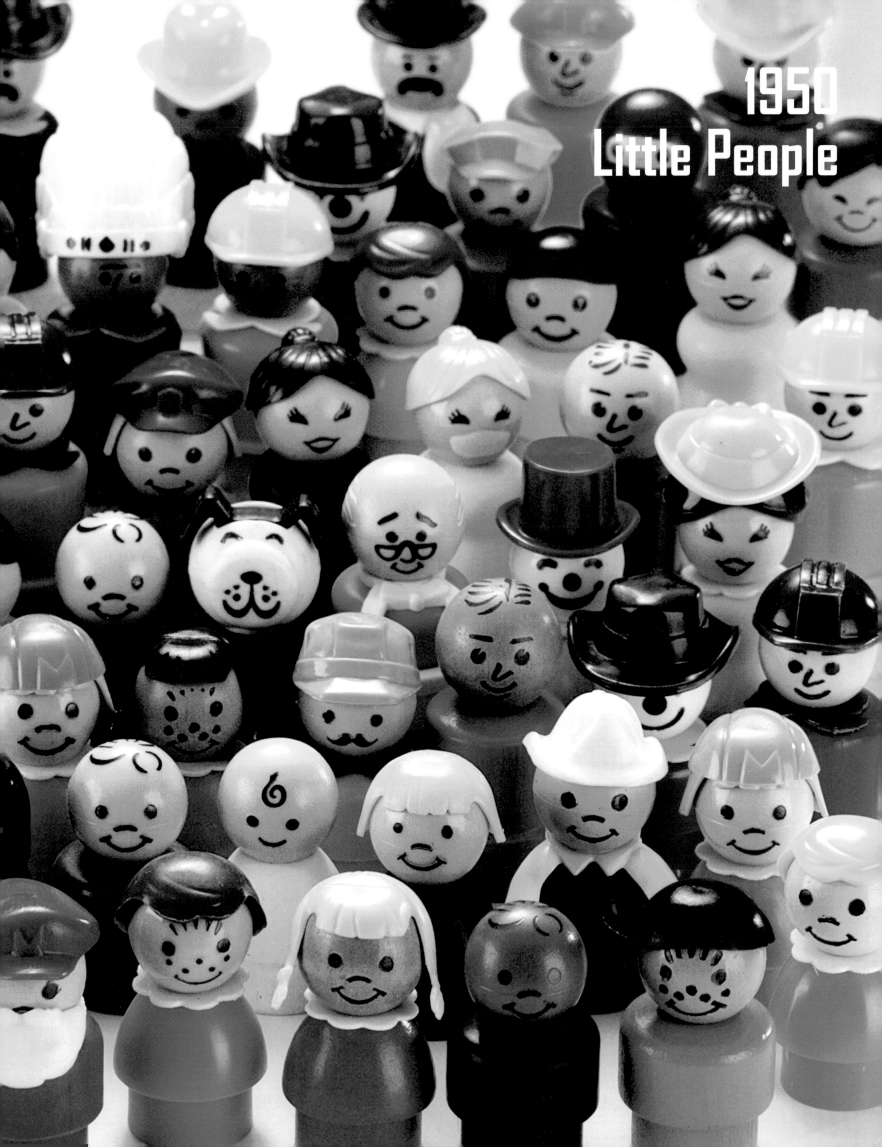

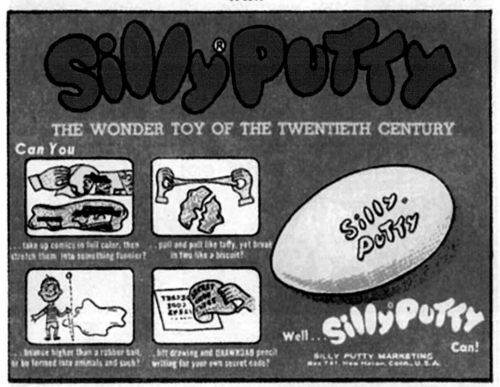

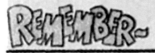 
104

World War II had a profound impact on the toy industry, and not always by design. Due to rationing and the absence of raw materials, chemists around the country were searching for synthetic alternatives. One desperately needed item was synthetic rubber. Working in 1943 in the General Electric labs, Scottish-born engineer James Wright combined boric acid and silicon oil. The mixture became a polymer and, to Wright's surprise and delight, bounced when dropped on the floor. For the next six years, General Electric tried to find practical applications for the putty, but to no avail.

But the bouncing putty was fun—at least that's what Ruth Fallgatter, owner of a New Haven, Connecticut, toy store thought. She contracted marketing consultant Peter Hodgson to sell it in her catalog. It did well, but Fallgatter was ultimately unimpressed. Hodgson bought the rights to the product and continued trying to market it.

Hodgson brought his creation, renamed Silly Putty, to the Toy Fair, where buyers and industry experts advised him to give up. But Hodgson, fortunately, refused and set about manufacturing Silly Putty himself, initially putting the one-ounce pieces in eggs because it was close to Easter, and he could save money by shipping the eggs in surplus egg boxes. The putty began appearing in department, novelty and bookstores.

In August of 1950, a write-up on the putty appeared in the *New Yorker's* "Talk of the Town" section—and within three days, Hodgson had orders for more than 250,000 eggs of Silly Putty. With the help of TV advertising, the market shifted and an adult novelty became a hit child's toy—great for bouncing, molding, stretching, biting and picking up pictures from the comics.

In the ensuing years, Silly Putty would go to the Moon, become a fixture around the world and, finally, be firmly established as a retro classic with more than two million eggs sold each year by the beginning of the twenty-first century. And Hodgson, who had to borrow $147 to go into his initial production, left an estate of $140 million at his death in 1976.

Working in 1943 in the General Electric labs, Scottish-born engineer James Wright combined boric acid and silicon oil. The mixture became a polymer and, to Wright's surprise and delight, bounced when dropped on the floor.

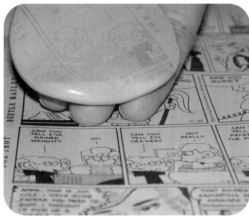

The fun of using Silly Putty to pick up and distort pictures from newspapers helped make it a hit

1951
Colorforms

Discovering that the vinyl stuck to the semi-gloss paint on their bathroom walls, Harry and Patricia Kislevitz, two art students, began cutting and decorating, even encouraging visitors to add their cutout creations to the wall.

Though vinyl had been around since the 1930s, it had largely been used for upholstery fabrics and other household items. But during World War II, vinyl sheeting was used to cover cables, to make them stronger and more water-resistant, and with the end of the war, sheet vinyl began appearing in all kinds of consumer products.

In 1951, Harry and Patricia Kislevitz, two art students, were given a new lightweight and more flexible vinyl that a friend was using to manufacture pocketbooks. Discovering that the vinyl stuck to the semigloss paint on their bathroom walls, they began cutting and decorating, even encouraging visitors to add their cutout creations to the wall.

Seeing the potential for a consumer product, the Kislevitzes launched what are now called Colorforms through FAO Schwarz, where they were an immediate hit. Colorforms were sold as an educational toy, and the first sets included basic shapes, letters and numbers. In 1962, Colorforms introduced Miss Weather, and with appearances on "Captain Kangaroo," she quickly became a top seller. Kids could use the Colorforms to dress up Miss Weather to be ready for whatever was going on outside.

It wasn't long before Colorforms began creating sets with popular cartoon characters and favorite stories. Over the years Barbie dolls, Mickey Mouse, "Sesame Street," Smurfs and even "The Dukes of Hazzard" and "The Addams Family" were featured in the sets. If it was on TV, chances are it showed up as a licensed Colorforms set.

Though the characters may have changed over the years, the simple open-ended play hasn't. As a springboard for the imagination, Colorforms remains a classic. The toy was even considered for the permanent design collection of the Museum of Modern Art.

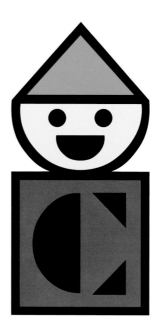

The famous Colorforms logo created by noted graphic designer Paul Rand

"They stick like magic!"

1951 Roy Rogers Cap Pistol

During the '30s and '40s, cowboys—and especially cowboys who could sing and shoot—were all the rage, and a whole generation of boys grew up wanting to trade in the ever-expanding suburban backyards for wide open spaces. Cowboys stars were the action heroes of the day, stalwart, true and always following the Cowboys Code, which was actually more about living honorably and doing the right thing than fighting the guys in the black hats.

Of all the cowboy stars, Roy Rogers was the biggest. He would star in 87 films and his TV series would run for six years, beginning December 30, 1951. Hopalong Cassidy, Gene Autry, Wyatt Earp, Wild Bill Hickock and others would influence the play of boys throughout the early 1950s.

To all make-believe backyard cowboy heroes (and an equal number of villains, generally played by younger brothers), Marx was the purveyor of choice. It was from Marx that they got their real-looking toy guns, holsters and all the accessories that let them win the West or at least the Western portion of the playground. The largest toy manufacturer in the U.S. in the years right after World War II, Marx made twenty percent of all the toys sold in the U.S. in the 1950s.

What mattered to kids, though, was that Marx supplied them with replicas of the guns their heroes, especially Roy Rogers, carried. Plus, thanks to roll caps (a toy developed right after the Civil War), kids could replicate the sound of blazing pistols and, at least in their imaginations, turn placid, postwar neighborhoods into dangerous Dead Rock Gulch.

"Lord, I reckon I'm not much just by myself, I fail to do a lot of things I ought to do. But Lord, when trails are steep and passes high, help me ride it straight the whole way through.

"And when in the falling dusk I get that final call, I do not care how many flowers they send. Above all else, the happiest trail would be for You to say to me, 'Let's ride, My Friend.' Amen."

—Roy Rogers Prayer

1951
Ginny Dolls

Jennie Adler Graves, a pioneer in plastics and sleep eyes in smaller dolls, invented Ginny. At first she didn't want to name the doll, thinking little girls should name their own dolls. Nonetheless, Ginny became a star.

Throughout the 1950s, there was one doll that most girls wanted and played with—Ginny. The Vogue Doll Company first used the name on an eight-inch doll in 1950, and it proved so popular that in 1951 all of their similar dolls were marketed under the Ginny name.

Of course, the doll changed a great deal over the decade, but she never really lost her essential baby or toddler look. (It would only be at the end of the decade that consumers would accept the notion that a doll could be—gasp!—a teenager.) Given how popular she was, Ginny and her world began to grow. In 1954 she got a walking mechanism, and by 1957 she was truly a play doll with bendable knees and a whole family of friends and accessories.

Today, the line is owned by the New Vogue Doll Company, and the focus is on the doll collector. Ginny's unique and cherished place among dolls is assured forever. She still has a special place in the hearts of many women who remember her from childhood, and she will always remain their favorite doll.

1952
Mr. Potato Head

When Mr. Potato Head first hit store shelves in 1952, he broke one of every mom's cardinal rules: "Don't play with your food!" George Lerner's original concept was intended to be a premium given away with cereal, but Hasbro bought it and instead turned it into one of the classic toys of the twentieth century.

Originally, the toy came with a bunch of parts and a Styrofoam potato, but kids quickly grabbed any vegetable in the kitchen to create their kooky characters, using eyes, mouths and more. When it was first launched, Mr. Potato Head even smoked a pipe—something he gave up in more health-conscious times.

Mr. Potato Head was also the first toy ever to be advertised on television, and he became so popular that Hasbro introduced a whole gang of fruit and vegetable friends for him—Oranges, Carrots, Peppers and Cucumbers—not to mention Mrs. Potato Head.

Kids who remember the original Mr. Potato Head tell stories of how their moms got tired of finding all their produce with little holes in it. Whether in response to this or not, in 1964, Mr. Potato Head got a plastic potato.

Something about creating his funny faces and moveable features has made him a permanent and whimsical part of American culture. And Mr. Potato Head has embraced his role as an icon of fun. He has been a spokesperson, run for mayor of Boise and was immortalized in Pixar's *Toy Story*. Just past his fiftieth birthday, this Spud for All Seasons is still going strong.

1952 Matchbox Cars

The old cliché "good things come in small packages" has been true for more than fifty years, at least when it comes to Matchbox cars. They were one of the first boys' collectible toys. Kids amassed these almost naturally, spending hours at their local dime stores looking at all the new models and dreaming of owning them, very much like grown-ups did with real cars.

Kids loved having pockets or pails full of Matchbox replica cars, known for their precise detail and affordability. Depending on the day or the mood, a child could be a hero with a fire truck or a millionaire with a Rolls Royce, or sometimes both at once. And lots of kids never grew up...at least when it came to their cars, which is one of the reasons that Matchbox cars have proved so enduring. Today, collectors number in the hundreds of thousands all around the world.

As huge as the Matchbox brand is, it had humble beginnings. The very first Matchbox car was created in 1952 by Jack Odell, who made a miniature car for his daughter to take to school. Using an army-surplus die-casting machine, Odell made a tiny prototype of the Diesel Road Roller, a large toy vehicle he designed with his partners, Rodney and Leslie Smith, in Lesney Products. Odell placed the small car in a matchbox-sized container and the name was born. In its first year, Matchbox made four different models, promoting the line as a "toy that is a complete toy" for under a dollar.

Over the ensuing half century, the Matchbox brand expanded around the globe and the company changed hands many times. Yet what has never been lost is the endless fascination and imaginary magic that children of all ages bring to these cars.

Originally, the toy came with a bunch of parts and a Styrofoam potato, but kids quickly grabbed any vegetable in the kitchen to create their kooky characters, using eyes, mouths and more.

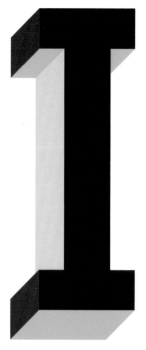

In popular images at least, it was the perfect time. Idealized families on television lived in immaculate Cape Cod houses in beautifully tailored suburbs. And for many in the culture, that was largely the case. With WWII over, the popular general Dwight Eisenhower in the White House and the Korean War far away, Americans were engaged in the biggest peacetime expansion ever. ■ Yet not everything was

"I Love Lucy" television show, c. 1955

completely halcyon, no matter how orderly the appearance. The cold war had erupted and fear of communism spread throughout the country. Senator Joseph McCarthy convened hearings and claimed to see traitors everywhere in government and the arts. In 1954, *Brown v. the Board of Education* ended segregation in schools and created many confrontations. Schoolchildren regularly participated in air-raid drills and would do so for the next decade, as if hiding under the desk or behind the lockers would protect against a dreaded H-bomb attack. ■ And all of this was brought into the home by television. For the first time technology allowed live coverage of events, so even those things that felt distant could be seen and heard in one's living room.

Drive-in movie theater, c. 1960

■ The growth of television was arguably one of the most important influences on the culture during this period. In addition to providing ideal

John F. Kennedy, c. 1960

family images on shows like "Father Knows Best," "The Adventures of Ozzie and Harriet" and others, television entertained the country with the antics of "I Love Lucy" and "The Honeymooners." For the first time there were shows especially created for kids as well, such as "The Mickey Mouse Club," and TV watching became a national pastime. TV began selling toys, and ads appeared for items like Mr. Potato Head, Silly Putty and toy gun sets based on the popular Westerns. News

1953-1962 The Ideal Family, the Baby Boom and the Rise of TV

broadcasts brought world events closer, which kept people glued to the set, and reporters like Edward R. Murrow and Walter Cronkite became household names. ■ Teenagers emerged as a social force, and the disaffected rebel became a popular image for boys, as embodied by movie stars James Dean and Marlon Brando. This was juxtaposed against the more clean-cut, preppy look with a flattop or crew cut. Women wore poodle skirts and ponytails, and for a while the coonskin cap was a fashion must. For the first time,

Baseball, 1962

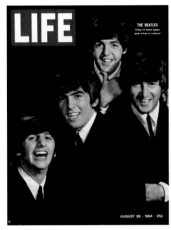

The Beatles, c. 1960s

teens proved their economic might, driving fads like the Hula Hoop.
■ This was the decade in which mass-market production and television began to play a major role in the toy industry. It was also a decade in which Westerns predominated and neighborhoods were overrun by cowboys and cowgirls. The Daisy Air Rifle was a much sought-after prize, as was the Howdy Doody doll, after the enormously popular TV show. Kids wore Davy Crockett hats and made funny faces with the magnetic Wooly Willy. Little brothers and sisters pushed around Fisher-Price's colorful, fascinating, clackety-clacking Corn Popper. Play sets became popular, with Fort Apache and Cape Canaveral creating a new type of figure-based play. Mattel had its first major hit with the mechanical Jack-in-the-Box, and near the end of the decade, the company would change dolls forever as paper fashion dolls gave way to the now ubiquitous Barbie doll. ■ The growing population of teenagers touched all elements of popular culture, especially music. And when Dick Clark took over hosting "American Bandstand" in 1956, the onetime local Philadelphia show

Elvis and his fans, 1956

became a national sensation, spreading rock 'n' roll and images of the carefree teenage lifestyle around the country. Radio shifted from entertainment programming, which had largely gone to television, to music, and helped create the fame of Elvis Presley, Bill Haley and the Comets and many other groups. The invention of the transistor radio meant that kids and adults had music most everywhere they went. ■ As the decade ended, the influence on youth and the youth culture would only get stronger, as the baby boomers were growing up. The hotly contested presidential election of 1960 made John F. Kennedy the youngest president ever elected. It was a time of great achievements— the first man in space, a narrowly averted war with Cuba— and many were confident that the American way of life was established forever. Nonetheless, the nation was on the brink of unforeseeable, permanent and revolutionary change.

Teenagers on motorcycle, 1962

Meet "The Flintstones," 1950s

1955 Gumby

This photo of Art Clokey's father was the inspiration for the lump on Gumby's head.

While certainly a cultural icon, it hasn't always been easy going for the character who "was once a little green ball of clay." Developed by animator Art Clokey, Gumby was first conceived for an animated jazz video, but studio heads thought he was much better for children.

So Clokey developed claymation cartoons starring Gumby and, subsequently, horse pal Pokey, dog Nopey and the "bad guy" Blockheads that were seen on "Howdy Doody" and later spun off into "The Gumby Show." The show didn't find an audience and lasted only a few months, but that was enough time for some toys to start filtering into the marketplace. Gumby very nearly languished in obscurity until the mid-60s, though, when the show was modestly successful in syndication—at least enough to inspire a new toy line of bendables based on Gumby and Pokey. Gumby might have disappeared again were it not for Eddie Murphy, who resurrected the character in a series of sketches for "Saturday Night Live" in the 1980s.

Still, what has made Gumby last despite all his setbacks has been the innocence he conveys and the essentially sweet, even if often illogical, storylines of his adventures. His unique look, Clokey has been quoted as saying, was inspired by a photograph of his father with a haircut with that odd bump on the side. Clokey thought that was funny and thought kids would, too.

Gumby lives on as an icon of kitsch and as one of the inspirations for many of the "out there" characters that have come after him.

123

1957
Cherry Twins

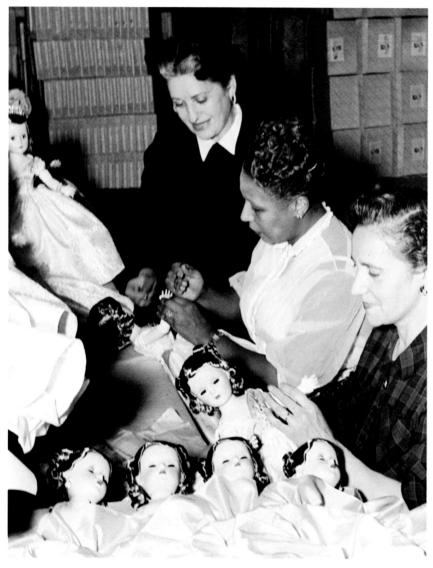

Madame Alexander herself oversaw production of the dolls; her attention to detail and eye for fashion helped create her signature looks

Throughout virtually all of the twentieth century, the doll industry in the United States has been shaped by the vision and innovation of one person—Beatrice "Madame" Alexander. In 1895, she was literally born into the business. Her father, Maurice, founded America's first doll hospital.

Beatrice herself entered the business in 1923, at her kitchen table, where she adopted the title "Madame." This title may have seemed quite grand for a woman of twenty-eight, but Beatrice was determined, and over the years she proved to be a brilliant businesswoman. In fact, she was as proud of her reputation as a shrewd executive as she was of being celebrated for quickly responding to and often being well ahead of styles, trends and what the public wanted.

In short, Madame virtually created the modern doll business. She was the first to make composition dolls with painted features and sleep eyes, using distinctive face molds, designing dolls with features and creating licensed dolls and dolls based on real people, long before it was a common practice. Madame was also the first manufacturer to use hard plastic.

Madame believed that "dolls should look like children and children should look like dolls." The idealized image of a little girl is what inspired her signature face sculpts, which became legendary and very much in demand, and can be seen in dolls such as the Cherry Twins. Other famous Madame creations were based on Scarlett O'Hara and the Dionne quintuplets.

Though considered as collectibles today, Madame Alexander dolls have always been popular for playing and display. They are exhibited in the Smithsonian and cherished by collectors of all ages. They have truly been the dolls everyone could love, and Madame's legacy of beauty, purity and goodness is still captured in every doll.

1956
Play-Doh

To baby boomers and every generation since, there is one smell that never fails to bring back happy memories—fresh Play-Doh.

There are various stories about how Play-Doh was created, but all agree that it had something to do with wallpaper; it wasn't originally intended as a toy at all. Noah and Joe McVicker apparently were looking for a compound that could be used as wallpaper cleaner. What they created during their experimentation was an off-white lump that seemed to do the trick, and so they took it to market—only later realizing that it could be modeled and played with. That's one story. Another story says the inspiration for developing Play-Doh as a toy came when Joe McVicker made the compound from wallpaper paste for his sister's preschool class.

One way or the other, Play-Doh was an instant hit with kids, and McVicker formed Rainbow Crafts to sell the modeling compound, packed in four cans in primary colors plus white, to department stores and schools in Cincinnati. Parents and teachers loved it, too, as it was one of the first real alternatives to oil-based clays and was reusable when stored correctly in its airtight container.

Kenner acquired the product from Rainbow Crafts, and soon everyone from Captain Kangaroo to Miss Frances of "Ding Dong School" was singing its praises as a new tool to inspire creativity. In 1960, Kenner introduced the Fun Factory, which allowed kids to extrude different shapes that could then be modeled. When Kenner was acquired by Hasbro, Play-Doh began being marketed under the Playskool brand. New products, new colors, even licensed sets followed, but no matter what innovation came along, that great smell is as fresh now as it was in 1956.

There are various stories about how Play-Doh was created, but all agree that it had something to do with wallpaper; it wasn't originally intended as a toy at all. Noah and Joe McVicker apparently were looking for a compound that could be used as wallpaper cleaner.

1957
Cherry Twins

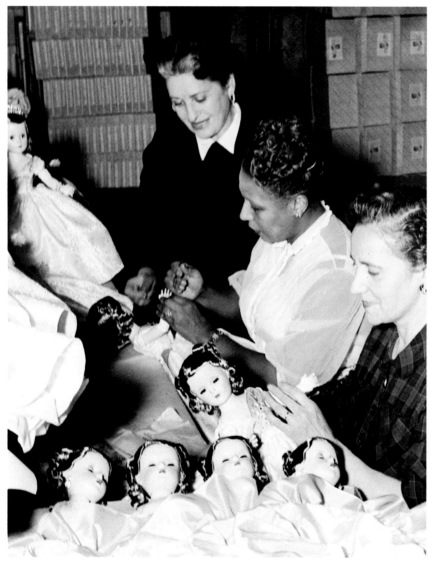

Madame Alexander herself oversaw production of the dolls; her attention to detail and eye for fashion helped create her signature looks

Throughout virtually all of the twentieth century, the doll industry in the United States has been shaped by the vision and innovation of one person—Beatrice "Madame" Alexander. In 1895, she was literally born into the business. Her father, Maurice, founded America's first doll hospital.

Beatrice herself entered the business in 1923, at her kitchen table, where she adopted the title "Madame." This title may have seemed quite grand for a woman of twenty-eight, but Beatrice was determined, and over the years she proved to be a brilliant businesswoman. In fact, she was as proud of her reputation as a shrewd executive as she was of being celebrated for quickly responding to and often being well ahead of styles, trends and what the public wanted.

In short, Madame virtually created the modern doll business. She was the first to make composition dolls with painted features and sleep eyes, using distinctive face molds, designing dolls with features and creating licensed dolls and dolls based on real people, long before it was a common practice. Madame was also the first manufacturer to use hard plastic.

Madame believed that "dolls should look like children and children should look like dolls." The idealized image of a little girl is what inspired her signature face sculpts, which became legendary and very much in demand, and can be seen in dolls such as the Cherry Twins. Other famous Madame creations were based on Scarlett O'Hara and the Dionne quintuplets.

Though considered as collectibles today, Madame Alexander dolls have always been popular for playing and display. They are exhibited in the Smithsonian and cherished by collectors of all ages. They have truly been the dolls everyone could love, and Madame's legacy of beauty, purity and goodness is still captured in every doll.

GUMBY
THE SUPER-FLEX

**WATCH THE
ADVENTURES
OF GUMBY
ON TELEVISION!**

You can animate
YOUR OWN GUMBY ADVENTURES
With this genuine
stop motion puppet!
3-D GUMBY animation booklet
available now
See coupon on
back of card.

NON-TOXIC   WASHABLE

PAT. PENDING   CREATED BY CLOKEY PRODUCTIONS, INC. CALIF.

1957
Frisbee

As with many hit toys, the Frisbee is surrounded by legend. Of course, flying disks used as playthings, sporting goods and weapons date back to the ancients. But most accounts of the invention of the Frisbee concur that it was inspired by the tossing of empty pie plates in and around Bridgeport, Connecticut. The pies came from the Frisbie Baking Company, and Yale is often cited as the first of many college campuses where tossing the (empty) pie plates was as good an excuse as any to avoid studying.

In 1948, Walter Frederick Morrison developed a plastic version, which allowed the disk to fly like a saucer, not wobble through the air like, well, a pie plate. He named it the Pluto Platter to capitalize on the then-current fascination with outer space and aliens. He sold his toy by giving demonstrations and touring college campuses, where it was a strong, but modest, success.

In 1955, Morrison teamed up with Arthur "Spud" Melin and Richard Knerr, who had just formed a company called Wham-O, and were marketing their first product—a slingshot. The disk was patented and production began in 1957. Knerr, by the way, is credited with renaming the toy "Frisbee," a phonetic spelling of the name of the pie company.

Frisbee would become a major hit. It wasn't marketed as a toy; it was promoted as a sport, and it was eagerly embraced by the public. Soon after its introduction, it was seen on beaches, in parks, virtually anywhere there was wide open space and eager fans could refine their throwing and catching techniques. In 1964, the first "professional" Frisbee was made, and in 1967, the game of Ultimate Frisbee was invented—a kind of cross between football, basketball and soccer. Later even Frisbee golf would become a recognized sport, and every year there would be national contests for the best Frisbee-catching dogs.

Frisbee was probably the first toy ever to have (almost) literally started as pie-in-the-sky, but since it took off, the game of catch has never been the same.

FRISBEE

1958
Hula Hoop

Once the craze hit, more than twenty-five million Hula Hoops were sold in the U.S. in four months.

We've all heard of fads spinning out of control. Well, that's literally what happened when the Hula Hoop hit the U.S. in 1958. Before the highest point of the craze spun itself out, in just four months, more than twenty-five million Hula Hoops had been sold, and not just to kids. Adults and teenagers loved them, too. It was the first fad that completely swept the nation, and it hit just at the time that the formality of the Eisenhower years was starting to loosen up. Rock and roll got people swinging their hips, and while they were at it, why not try to keep a plastic hoop revolving around one's midsection, or other body parts for that matter? At the zenith of the phenomenon, even adults competed to see how many hoops they could keep going and for how long.

The guys behind the Hula Hoop were Arthur "Spud" Melin and Richard Knerr, founders of Wham-O. They had seen children in Australia playing with bamboo hoops as part of a gym class. It looked like fun, so the partners decided to make hoops out of plastic and sell them as toys. They called them Hula Hoops because the gyrations of the hips required to keep the swirling rings aloft looked a lot like the Hawaiian dance, and the exotic islands were very popular at the time.

The Hula Hoop wasn't an instant hit, however, so as they had done before with their Frisbee, Melin and Knerr hit the streets, giving away products and encouraging kids to try them at playgrounds throughout Southern California. It was slow going at first and then, bang! "Hoop-de-doo," one might say.

The Hula Hoop was helped greatly by the growing national media. Television, magazines and newspapers all jumped into the ring with great visuals, all of which seemed to convey just how much fun the Hula Hoop was.

Playing with a hoop was nothing new. Hoops had been used for sports and recreation throughout history. Colonial children played with barrel hoops, a game that persisted into the early twentieth century. So what made the Hula Hoop such a remarkable success? It was the combination of youthful exuberance, the spirit of the times, a simple idea and an enthusiastic media that created a sensation that has never been matched since.

The Wham-O factory, San Gabriel, California, 1958: Wham-O worked hard to keep up with demand once the Hula Hoop craze hit, adding manufacturing facilities in Chicago, London, Tokyo, Paris and Toronto

1959 Barbie Dolls

Though her measurements have been a source of conversation for decades, Barbie Millicent Rogers (her real name) is shaped the way she is largely because she's easy for little girls to dress.

There has never been and never will be a toy like the Barbie doll. It has been an icon almost since its introduction in 1959. An American institution, the Barbie doll has shaped the play, imagination and lives of millions and millions of girls around the world, reflecting their hopes and dreams. And, in fact, she's been whatever anyone wanted to make of her. Quite a lot for the quintessential American teen to handle, but those little plastic shoulders have always been something more than meets the eye.

The Barbie doll was the brainchild of Ruth Handler. In the 1950s, there was no such thing as a hard-plastic "fashion doll." There were baby dolls, mostly, but the only dolls that let girls play with fashion were paper dolls. As Handler watched her daughter, Barbara, and friends play with them, she thought there needed to be a three-dimensional fashion doll for these girls, who, she realized, were acting out their futures as adult women. Handler came to believe passionately that this kind of play would help girls build their self-esteem.

Handler took her idea for a molded fashion doll to the marketing executives at her company, Mattel, but they rejected it, saying that dolls should all be babies. Soon after, on a trip to Europe, though, Handler found the inspiration for the doll that she had envisioned. First introduced in Germany in 1955, it was a doll named Lilli. Lilli confirmed Handler's belief that there was a market for a doll that represented a real grown-up, and a very beautiful one too, with a whole wardrobe of fashionable clothing. Bringing Lilli back to the States, she created a new design for dolls—slim, attractive and eleven inches tall. She convinced Mattel to launch the doll, even hiring designer Charlotte Johnson to create a line of clothes for the new doll, now named Barbie in honor of Handler's daughter.

The Barbie doll was unveiled at the Toy Fair in 1959. While not an instant hit with the toy trade, little girls loved her, and the first year's sales of the dolls topped 350,000 units at a retail price of three dollars each. That was incredible at the time but nowhere near the nearly $2 billion annual business she would become near the end of the century.

The Barbie doll's special magic has always been the way in which she reflected the world, the aspirations and the possibilities of little girls. The Barbie doll changed as the world changed. As women's roles and opportunities expanded, so did the Barbie doll's. Virtually reinvented in the '70s, the Barbie doll regained her iconic status as a girl who could do anything—anything, that is, a little girl could imagine. She's been to the Moon, she's been a doctor, a teacher and, just as Ruth Handler hoped, a springboard for imagination and dreams.

What will the Barbie doll be tomorrow? No one can be completely sure, but as long as little girls dream, the Barbie doll will be there to help them realize those dreams through play.

By 1964 Trolls had taken over the world of toy sales, as well as the hearts of kids everywhere

1959 Trolls

In the early 1960s, Trolls were one must-have collectible for girls and boys alike. And it wasn't just kids. Trolls were everywhere: rock bands and even the first lady were being photographed with the odd-looking dolls.

In fact, for a while, Trolls were so popular that only the Barbie doll sold more pieces—and you couldn't imagine two more dissimilar looks, though both had plenty of outfits. (They didn't share.)

Trolls, so the legend goes, come from Scandinavia. They are mythic little creatures who live in the woods, grant wishes and are basically into good times without too many cares. No wonder they were popular with the emerging youth culture in the U.S. in the early 1960s.

The dolls that started the trend were created by Thomas Dam in Denmark. Originally carved from wood, they were later manufactured in plastic and sold in the U.S. under the Wishnik brand name. With Trolls, it was always a bad hair day, and that was part of their appeal. Their unusual looks, characterized by wrinkled faces, big ears and silly, happy grins, made them unlike any other dolls on the market.

Trolls were so popular that pretty soon other companies began producing their own versions, and they would experience several waves of popularity throughout the remainder of the century. In 1987, Russ Berrie, in particular, built a huge business on Trolls, manufacturing them in a variety of sizes and themes. For toys and gifts, there was a Troll for virtually every occasion.

For a while, Trolls were so popular that only the Barbie doll sold more pieces—and you couldn't imagine two more dissimilar looks, though both had plenty of outfits. (They didn't share.)

In the late 1980s Trolls made a big comeback; this 1992 version was made by Russ Berrie & Company

1959 Chatty Cathy

Like many dolls of the period, Chatty Cathy, introduced in 1959, was all about dress-up play, and she would become iconic in her own way as a favorite of a generation of girls. Chatty Cathy had a very chic wardrobe and came in a variety of hair and eye colors and even an African-American version.

But what made her so very special was that for the first time a girl's doll could talk back to her. There had been Ma-Ma dolls before, but Cathy was the first doll to really talk to her make-believe mommies (with a pull of her string). And talk she did, saying eleven different things, including "Let's play house," "Please change my dress," "Tell me a story" and "I love you." Little girls fell in love with the beautifully sculpted doll, and she is still one of the toys most fondly recalled by baby boomers. In fact, lovingly tucked away in many an adult woman's closet is her original Chatty Cathy—often the only toy preserved from childhood. And she still talks.

Cathy's original voice was recorded by June Foray, who also was the voice of Rocky the Flying Squirrel in "The Adventures of Rocky and Bullwinkle." (When Mattel reintroduced the doll in the 1970s, the voice was provided by Maureen McCormick—known to a generation as Marcia Brady from "The Brady Bunch." McCormick also appeared in TV commercials for the doll.)

The talking feature proved so popular that in 1962 Mattel introduced Singing Chatty Cathy and went on to give her a big sister, Charmin' Chatty, and a little sister, Chatty Baby.

By the end of the century, virtually every doll talked, and the conversations, powered by computer chips, extended to hundreds of phrases. But no single doll ever spoke so compellingly to a generation of little girls or would capture the imagination of the culture in the way Chatty Cathy did.

MATTEL
DOLLS 1960

PLEASE CARRY ME

I LOVE YOU

I'M HUNGRY

I GOT HURT

TELL ME A STORY

I CAN REALLY TALK!

WILL YOU PLAY WITH ME?

PLEASE BRUSH MY HAIR

WHERE ARE WE GOING?

CHANGE MY DRESS

I'M ALL TIRED

MATTEL, INC. TOYMAKERS

NOW—
...THE SEN-"SAY"-TIONAL CONVERSATION DOLL!

SHE SAYS 11 PHRASES AT RANDOM!

She speaks for herself. With each pull of the magic ring, she talks like a real little girl . . . little girls can **converse** with Chatty Cathy*. Laboratory-use-tested voice unit has 90-day factory warranty. Chatty Cathy* **looks** real . . . she's 20" tall with movable head, arms and legs; her blonde rooted hair can be brushed and arranged. Her flesh-tone body is realistically proportioned and contoured. Chatty Cathy*, fully clothed in a removable dress is available in two different outfits, as described below.

STOCK #682. Retail Price: $18.00. Chatty Cathy* in a cute red pinafore . . . remove it and she's dressed in a matching red play suit! Colorful satin hair ribbon, white cotton socks and red velvet shoes — all removable. Individually packaged in a portable suitcase-type box with carrying handle. A colorful 8-page Story Book is also included. **Size: 20" high. Std. Pack: 3/12 doz. Wt., 11½ lbs.**

STOCK #681. Retail Price: $18.00. Chatty Cathy* in a blue cotton party dress with eyelet shorty blouse, panties, petticoat, satin hair ribbon, white cotton socks and blue velvet shoes. Remove her shorty blouse, and she's wearing a blue play dress! Individually packaged in suitcase-type box with carrying handle. Colorful 8-page Chatty Cathy* Story Book included. **Size: 20" high. Std. Pack: 3/12 doz. Wt., 11½ lbs.**

Chatty Cathy
THE TALKING DOLL!

I'm MATTEL's
Chatty Cathy
I CAN REALLY TALK!

Ask to hear me...
I can say lots of
things as we play
together!

TV ADVERTISED

CHATTY CATHY* DOLL ASSORTMENT

STOCK #688. Retail Value: $108.00.
The most talked about doll assortment of 1960, planned to provide a balanced minimum stock, to sell itself. Consists of 3/12 doz. #682 Chatty Cathy* dolls, in red pinafore dress, etc. 3/12 doz. #681 Chatty Cathy* dolls, in blue party dress plus

1960
Mr. Machine

They called him "the modern take-apart robot with a Personality!" And for millions of kids during the 1960 holidays, Mr. Machine's arm-swinging walk, chomping mouth, dinging bell and siren that rang every fifteen seconds made him the must-have toy of the season.

His catchy jingle became a song nearly every kid could sing:
"Here he comes, here he comes, greatest toy you've ever seen. And his name is Mr. Machine. He is real. He is real. And for you, he is Ideal. And his name is Mr. Machine. MR. MACHINE! MR. MACHINE!!!"

Partly as a result of this infectious tune, Mr. Machine became one of the first toys in the 1960s to be widely known in the culture at large. It also helped establish Ideal as one of the largest toy companies of the time.

Mr. Machine was designed by Marvin Glass, who, in addition to being a member of the Toy Industry Hall of Fame, was one of the most prolific and successful toy designers of this period. From 1949 through 1974, he created some of the classics of the twentieth century, including Mystery Date, Time Bomb, Lite Brite, Rock 'Em Sock 'Em Robots, Operation, Tipit, Toss Across and many more.

Mr. Machine was the perfect toy for a culture obsessed with robotics and education. Though it was mostly entertaining, the toy was promoted as educational, since kids could use the plastic wrench to take it apart and put it back together again, ostensibly learning about gears and machinery. Mostly, though, they liked to turn the key and watch Mr. machine walk while his gears turned merrily. And happily for parents, he came fully assembled.

Ideal would extend the brand into a popular game and reissue a new Mr. Machine in 1977. Though it never achieved the level of popularity it had in the 1960s, the toy became a classic and today is considered highly collectible.

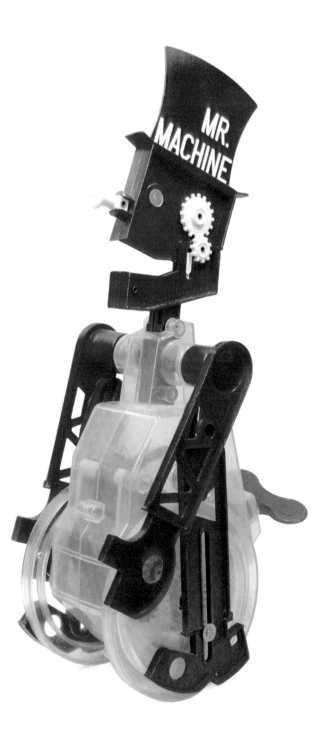

Though it was mostly entertaining, the toy was promoted as educational, since kids could use the plastic wrench to take it apart and put it back together again, ostensibly learning about gears and machinery.

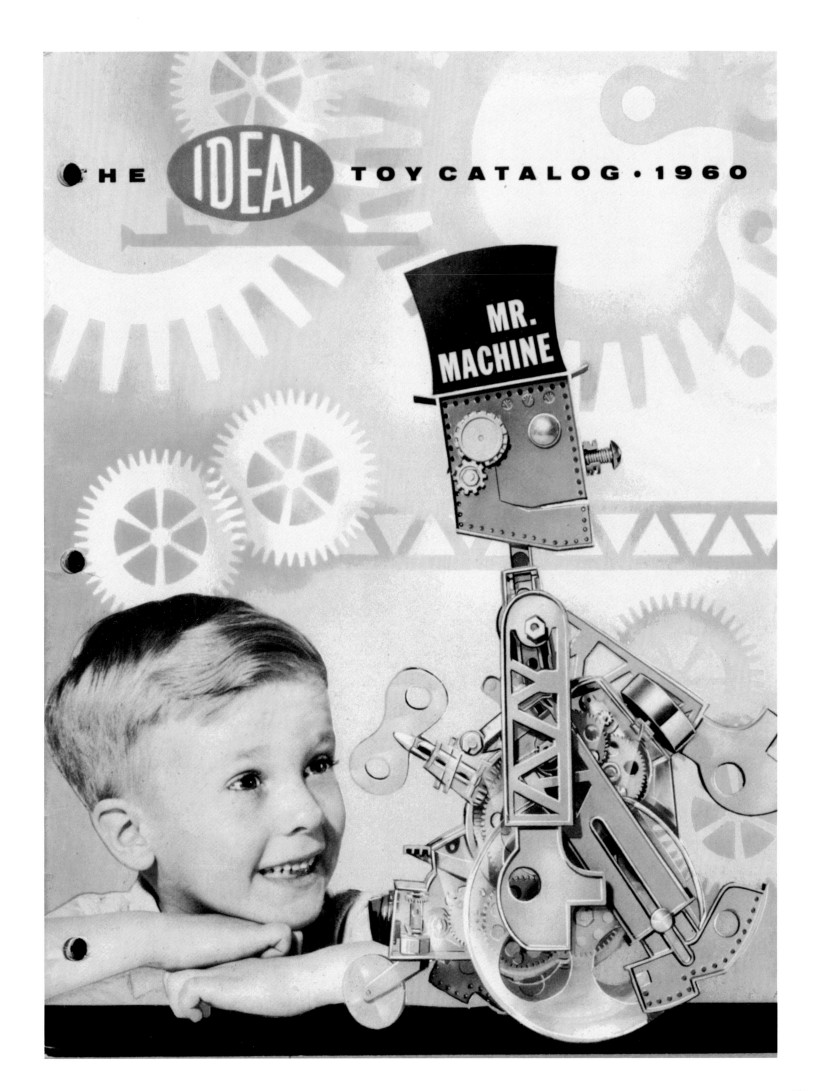

THE **IDEAL** TOY CATALOG · 1960

MR. MACHINE

1960
Wooden Railway

By 2002, the company was producing 3.5 million train cars, 14 million wheels and 9 million pieces of track. That's enough track to build a BRIO railway between New York and Chicago.

In the early 1960s, most American toys were a celebration of plastic. Bright, colorful, inexpensive and profitable, plastic represented the new, the now and the modern. Yet across the Atlantic, in Sweden, a company that had been manufacturing classic wooden toys since 1884 was introducing a product that in the coming years would help shape the U.S. specialty toy market.

A family company, BRIO derived its name from BRothers Ivasson at Osby, the town where the company had been making toys for seventy-six years when they introduced their classic wooden train set.

The set was a hit, with its finely carved tracks and magnetic connectors to hold the tracks together. A few made it to the United States to be sold in small stores that specialized in international toys, but without broad-based distribution, the sets and BRIO were not widely known. There were some wooden and plastic train sets made by smaller manufacturers for U.S. distribution during this period, but nothing as sophisticated as the BRIO sets.

That changed in 1977 when BRIO began distributing in the U.S. The lines became a staple of specialty stores, and the classic simplicity and precise engineering of the sets would have a huge impact on design in preschool toys both for the specialty and the mass markets, helping establish a new sensitivity toward toy design throughout the industry.

By the end of the century, BRIO was an established toy line in the United States with a strong following and many fans. And by 2002, the company was producing 3.5 million train cars, 14 million wheels and 9 million pieces of track. Incidentally, that's enough track to build a BRIO railway between New York and Chicago.

1960
Etch A Sketch

What's inside? Here's the secret: The knobs control a network of strings that guides a stylus as it literally etches images in the aluminum powder that coats the screen. Turn it over and shake it, and the powder fills in the lines. Magic!

In 1960, Ohio Art kept its assembly line running until noon on December 24 to try to meet the demand for its hit product—Etch A Sketch. Developed in France by Arthur Granjean in the late 1950s, "L'Ecran Magique" (the Magic Crayon) was brought to the U.S., where it was given a new name and became an instant sensation. By the end of the century, millions had been sold in nearly seventy countries worldwide.

Etch A Sketch is still completely assembled by hand. Production took place in Bryan, Ohio, until the end of 2000, when it was moved to Asia, making Etch A Sketch one of the last toys to be fully produced in the U.S. Nonetheless, the toy has remained unchanged, and its red frame and two knobs have become iconic for almost three generations.

But what's inside? Here's the secret: The knobs control a network of strings that guides a stylus as it literally etches images in the aluminum powder that coats the screen. Turn it over and shake it, and the powder fills in the lines. Magic! Or at least pretty close.

While most people are able to draw squares and squiggles, many artists have refined their talent to the point where they can create truly amazing artwork. Like many things in life, it simply requires practice.

Stud-and-tube
construction gave
LEGO's "Automatic
Binding Bricks"
greater stability
and allowed larger
models to be built.

LEGO arrives in the U.S. as part of the
1961 Macy's Thanksgiving Day parade

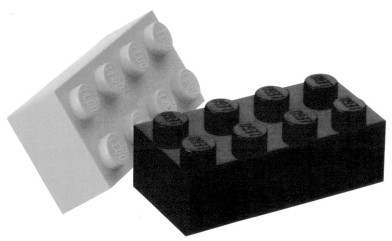

In the latter part of the twentieth century, countless kids spent Saturdays, rainy days and even sick days building with LEGO bricks. Few toys have been as popular or created as many imaginative opportunities or wonderful memories for children. Playing with LEGO, in fact, is all about imagination; it's about seeing a model first in the mind's eye and then creating it—perhaps one of the most beneficial elements of play. Of course, kids don't necessarily see that. What they love is building!

The LEGO Company was begun in 1932 in Billund, Denmark, by Ole Kirk Christiansen. The company made a variety of wooden home products as well as toys. Two years later, the toy line was dubbed LEg GOdt ("play well"). Later, it was realized that in Latin the word means "I study" or "I put together." In 1947, the company purchased the first injection-molding machine in Denmark and added plastic toys, called Automatic Binding Bricks, to its wood line. Over the next eight years, the company developed and perfected these bricks, now known as LEGO Bricks, and expanded distribution into Germany. In 1958, the stud-and-tube construction system, which allowed greater stability and larger models, was patented and new parts were added to the sets.

LEGO finally made it to the U.S. in 1961, and was quickly embraced by parents and kids. There had been building toys before—even brick-based building toys—but none of them held together or allowed such diversity in model construction.

Throughout the rest of the century, LEGO would grow and expand, becoming an integral part of children's lives—both boys and girls. The bricks themselves never changed, and were handed down from parents to kids. Theme parks sprung up around the world, licenses would boost sales and the bricks would even enter the robotic age with a complete line of products and a play lab at Massachusetts Institute of Technology.

But what would never change would be LEGO's commitment to learning, play and child development—as well as that moment of magic when a child first begins to build with LEGO bricks.

1962 Chatter Telephone

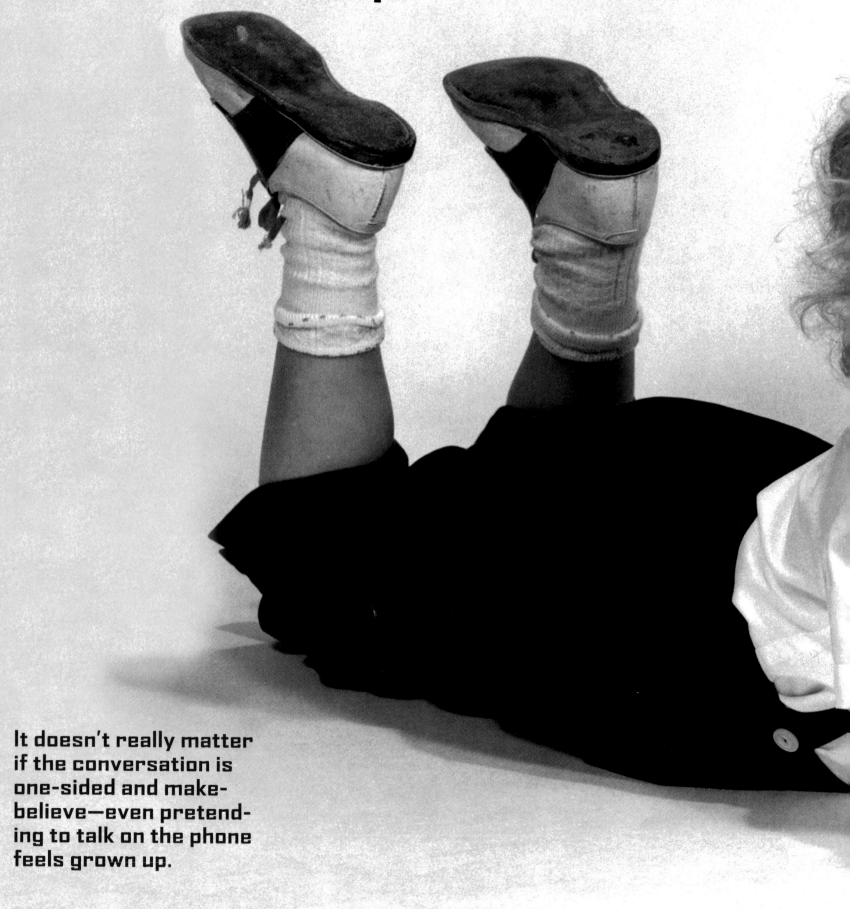

It doesn't really matter if the conversation is one-sided and make-believe—even pretending to talk on the phone feels grown up.

There's nothing preschoolers want to do so much as imitate adults. And one of the classic play patterns has always been talking on the telephone, just like mom and dad. For toddlers, it doesn't really matter if the conversation is one-sided and completely make-believe—even pretending to talk on the phone feels grown up.

There had been toy telephones before, but in 1961, Fisher-Price combined its huge success in pull-toys with cute character design and a basic phone to create the Talk Back Telephone, but it didn't sell. Bruce Fox of Fisher-Price says, "Perhaps because the times were more innocent, parents didn't want to buy something that would encourage their children to 'talk back.'" In 1962, Fox says, the name was changed to the Chatter Telephone, and a classic was born.

Preschoolers loved the smiley face and the expressive eyes that moved as they tugged the toy around. When they sat to play, the clicking dial made them feel very grown-up. In fact, by the end of the century, Fisher-Price had sold more than thirty-five million of the toys. It had gone through some design modifications, but it was still the same lovable phone it had always been.

In the late 1990s, Fisher-Price redesigned the Chatter Phone to be a push-button phone, like the ones today's preschoolers see in their homes. But despite the realism, Fox says, sales weren't as strong. "We tried to bring it to the new millennium, but the concept is timeless," he concludes. Fisher-Price reintroduced the original version, and sales shot back up. The push-button version is still available, but parents and gift-givers, it seems, want the original.

No matter that the Chatter Telephone may be the only rotary phone today's children will ever use, it goes to show you can't mess with success.

149

As the 1960s dawned, Americans had no idea how profoundly the decade would permanently change everything in their culture—politics, entertainment, media, fashion, even childhood. Postwar affluence had created a sense that life was, and would always be—at least in the United States—comfortable and secure. ■ The election of John F. Kennedy in 1960 heralded the Sixties as a celebration of youth, possibility, hope and a shining future that was all but guaranteed—and that would look pretty much the way the architects of the booming suburbs and strip malls and television envisioned. And it was true, in a way. Youth would dominate the cul-

Twiggy, 1966

ture, but it would be a sometimes uneasy process of transformation and revolution, punctuated by celebration and the excitement of the new—a carnival of contradictions and change every-

1963-1972 The Times They Are A-Changin'

where. ■ The children who began the decade hiding under their desks during air-raid drills would end it marching on campuses to protest what they called a senseless war. For the first time, youth would set the political agenda, shifting the cultural focus forever to the younger generations. Timothy Leary "turned on, tuned in and dropped out," and experimentation with marijuana and psychedelic drugs would touch every part of the culture. From the repression and standardized roles of previous decades would emerge the sexual revolution. ■ The struggle for racial equality would boil over, and the assassinations of John F. Kennedy, Martin Luther King Jr., Malcolm X and Robert Kennedy would

Woodstock music festival, Bethel, New York, 1969

plunge the nation into grief and bring civil rights to the forefront of the nation's consciousness. The cold war meant that spies might be anywhere. Space would seem like an extension of our collective backyard, as man first orbited the Earth and then walked on the Moon. Everything was swept along in a wave of constant change that was exhilarating and unprecedented. ■ But it was also a time of fun and freedom, as though after the straitlaced Eisenhower years, everyone could finally relax. Seventy million teenagers and their high spirits influenced every aspect of the culture. The Beatles and the British Invasion changed the sound of popular music forever. Later, they would open the door to Eastern thought, meditation and a new way of being.

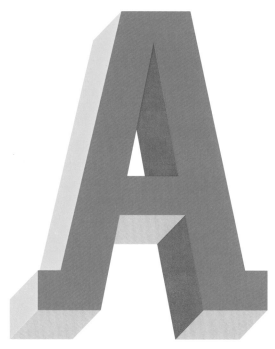

Suburban skater boys, 1960s

Even staid old Broadway felt the beat as *Hair* revolutionized the musical. Music would evolve rapidly throughout the decade,

Chubby Checker, 1960s

expanding the message of youth, love and freedom, which finally all came together during Woodstock in 1969. ■ Fashion went wild with Mary Quant and the miniskirt, Carnaby Street and white lipstick. The Nehru jacket and love beads were, briefly, the thing for swinging guys. Twiggy was the new face of 1966, establishing the look of the decade. Hippies created their own style, liberating even fashion, so granny glasses and go-go boots existed side by side in compatible disharmony. ■ Environmental awareness began with Rachel Carson's *Silent Spring*. Ralph Nader started the consumer activist movement. James Bond films, *The Sound of*

Sean Connery as "007," James Bond, 1964

Music and *Dr. Strangelove* were playing at the movies, along with *Midnight Cowboy* and *The Graduate*. Movies would become more political and explicit, prompting the introduction of the ratings code. ■ On TV, families tuned into "Bewitched," "I Dream of Jeannie" and "The Addams Family," along with the prime-time cartoons "The Flintstones" and "The Jetsons." "Laugh-In" established a new, fast-paced brand of comedy, while "Sesame Street" helped kids get ready to read. Children grew up in the glow of the television, and nearly 140 different television shows were created just for them. With kids tuned in to just three networks every Saturday, toy manufacturers could introduce their products to a nationwide audience all at once. New toys became a hot topic, and for the first time word of mouth was a powerful force in driving toy sales. ■ And what toys they were! The skill-and-action game revitalized the board-game category, with Mousetrap,

Unisphere, New York World's Fair, 1964–1965

Crazy Clock, Operation, Fascination, Skittle Bowl and Booby Trap. Kenner introduced its Girders and Panels for aspiring architects, and young showmen made the Give-A-Show Projector a hit. "High performance" was one of the watchwords of the era as Superballs bounced everywhere, the low-slung, plastic Big Wheel became a preferred mode of transportation, and Mattel's Whizzer Tops spun out. With the walk

Fashion models, 1971

on the Moon, space inspired imaginative play in the form of Major Matt Mason, as well as science kits. It was also a time of whimsy, creativity and fun like never before and, like everything during this period, slightly more intense and larger than life. ■ Media changed the world as news, tastes, trends and ideas covered the globe faster than at any other time in history, and we learned it really was a small world after all.

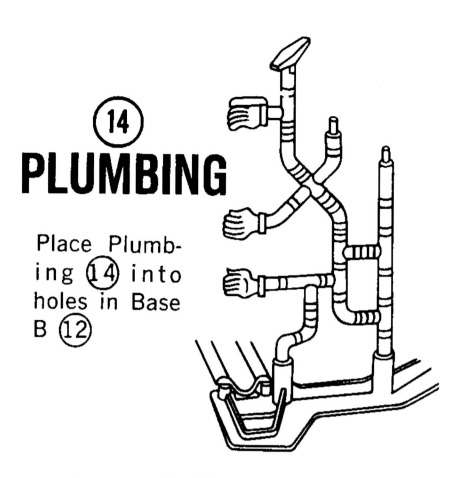

14 PLUMBING

Place Plumbing ⑭ into holes in Base B ⑫

"A game of zany action on a crazy contraption!"

It was not a better mousetrap that Ideal set out to build in 1963, but a hilarious game that would entertain kids with a kooky contraption in the style of Rube Goldberg, designed by Marvin Glass. Glass, who had previously designed Mr. Machine, King Zor and other hits of the early 1960s, was inspired by Goldberg's cartoon "Inventions," which had been hugely popular since it first began appearing in 1914. By the early '60s, "Rube Goldberg" had entered the American lexicon as a way of describing anything that used maximum effort to achieve minimal results.

But Glass took the hilarity one step further — he made it dimensional so it would really work. Players took turns adding pieces to the contraption as they moved their mice around the board. When the trap was finally built, you didn't want to land on the cheese space when another player landed on "Turn Crank," for that was his or her opportunity to set the machine going with rolling balls, swinging hands and even a diver going into a tub. If all went according to plan, your mouse was trapped and you were out of the game. But like a true Rube Goldberg machine, half the fun

was that even when built correctly, the mousetrap could misfire...and the game could go on and on. Though it was designed for and marketed to kids, many adults remember delightedly playing the game as families, and a whole new era of appreciation for Rube Goldberg was born.

The success of Mousetrap also signaled the beginning of the golden years for skill-and-action games. Marvin Glass would design many of those that became classics. There's just something about one's opponent running afoul of falling marbles (Ker-Plunk), finger-endangering snapping action (Booby Trap), races against time where the loser is "blown up" (Time Bomb, Dynamite Shack) and "wild animals" (Jungle Hunt) that remains inherently hilarious.

1963
Easy-Bake
Oven

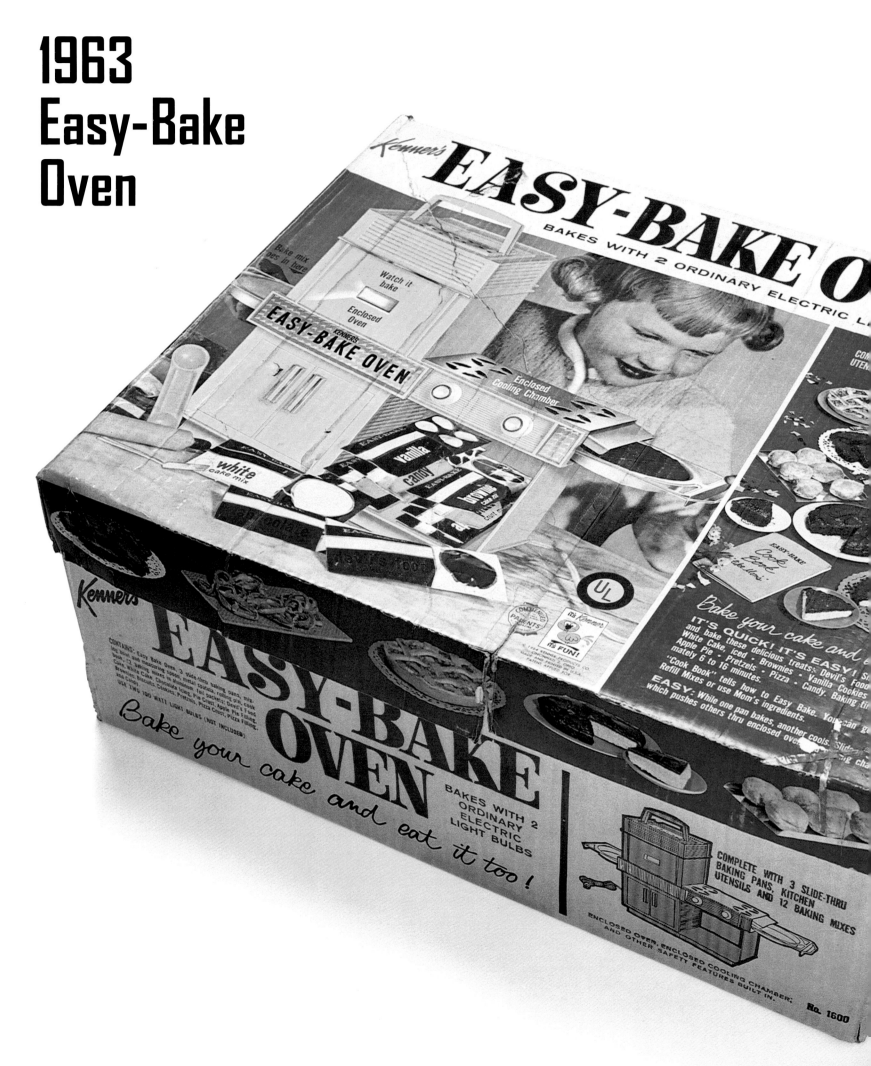

Outside of the Barbie doll, there is probably no more iconic girls' toy of the 1960s than the Easy-Bake Oven. Debuting in 1963 with a retail price of only $15.95, the aqua oven let every little girl be in charge of the kitchen.

Using four-inch pans, teeny cake-mix packets, water and the all-important light bulb, a whole generation of baby boomer girls had their first independent baking experiences with the Easy-Bake Oven. Easy-Bake tested a variety of different concoctions. In 1966, Kenner introduced a bubble-gum set, but it's always the cakes and brownies that bring back the memories, and who could forget the homey smell of a cake rising over a 60-watt bulb?

There was something about the Easy-Bake Oven that was just right for the time. Women's magazines were full of easy recipes, and packaged foods and mixes were proliferating on store shelves, so it only made sense that girls, who at the time foresaw a life of great food prepared with the utmost convenience, should want to mimic their moms with their very own kid-sized appliances.

Of course, the cakes were a little too small to provide dessert for the family—not that they weren't served. They were, however, just the right size for pretend tea parties at which the hostess ate the whole thing, perhaps sharing a bit with other human guests, but leaving nothing for the assembled dolls and teddy bears.

Over the years, the Easy-Bake Oven became a classic item. It is among the most cherished toys of girls who grew up with it, and it inspired the career of more than one pastry chef. And, like every good appliance, it has always been stylish, appearing over the years in avocado green, harvest gold, white, aqua and other colors. It's been styled as a contemporary range and a microwave, as well.

Now, according to today's moms who remember only too well, the mixes taste a heck of a lot better than they did originally. But it's anyone's guess if the products of the Easy-Bake Oven were ever really tasted for what they were, for it was the pride of being able to cook all by herself that invariably sweetened the result for the little girls who loved their Easy-Bake Ovens—and the recipients of the treats who loved those little girls.

Before G.I. Joe, there was no such thing as an action figure. In 1962, Don Levine, at the time the creative director for Hasbro, was approached about creating children's toys based on an upcoming TV series, "The Lieutenant." Though intrigued, Levine determined that the show was not really for kids and passed on the proposal.

But the idea for a soldier didn't go away. As Vincent Santelmo describes in *The Complete Encyclopedia to G.I. Joe*, it was a small wooden artist's mannequin that convinced Levine that a soldier figure could sell, particularly because of the popularity of soldiers at the time.

Levine sold the concept to Hasbro and development continued. Since the play would be all about action, it would have "21 movable parts," which would allow boys to engage in the kind of active play that would make this more than a doll.

Of course, the real problem was how to sell what was essentially a doll to boys. Hasbro positioned the figure, now called G.I. Joe, as a fighting man, and in advance of the Toy Fair in 1964 produced one of the first sales films shown to buyers at the New York trade show. Nonetheless, the response was lukewarm, and with more than two years of development and millions of dollars invested, G.I. Joe's fate was unclear.

But then, as often happens, kids heard about the toy and wanted it. Slowly at first, they started asking for G.I. Joe. That asking sold nearly $18 million worth of G.I. Joes and the necessary gear in the first year alone. Eventually, two out of three boys would have a G.I. Joe, and the line would represent 70 percent of Hasbro's business.

Things would certainly change as the decade went on. For one, the Vietnam conflict would put even more focus on combat toys. The line would expand, more soldiers would be added to the playground platoons and G.I. Joe would even talk.

1964 G.I. Joe

Before G.I. Joe, there was no such thing as an action figure.

As the political landscape changed, so did G.I. Joe. Throughout the 1970s, he would become a Real American Hero. In 1982, now a three-inch action figure like the *Star Wars* figures from Kenner, Joe began to do battle with his evil, if abstract, nemesis, Cobra. The Reagan years saw a change in attitude about the military, and a popular TV show provided plenty of story lines. G.I. Joe kept growing, and Hasbro introduced new themes for Joe's adventures every year. He was going to space, tracking mummies, doing virtually anything cool and adventure-oriented. He even developed martial arts powers, becoming a ninja. It was a long way from the army, air force, navy and marines, where he'd started.

Old soldiers may fade away, but not G.I. Joe. Oh sure, he's had his ups and downs. But whatever kids' tastes, G.I. Joe will always be popular with the huge and loyal collector community.

In the mid-90s, reflecting a new interest in the military, particularly historic figures, Hasbro introduced a special series of G.I. Joes. In 2002, G.I. Joe was matched up again with Cobra and moved back onto the toy battlefield. And in the wake of 9/11, G.I. Joe became an emblem of a nation's pride and power and was more relevant than ever.

1965
See 'n Say

See 'n Say was eagerly embraced by parents as an educational toy, and it set the stage for much of the development of educational toys that would occur over the next decades.

You can probably blame it on Chatty Cathy. The success of the talking doll, first launched in 1959, made talking toys all the rage, and in the early 1960s manufacturers scrambled to leverage the magical pull-string into other kinds of toys. Educational toys were a natural application because parents were increasingly concerned about their kids getting a jump on school.

See 'n Say was eagerly embraced by parents as an educational toy, and it set the stage for much of the development of educational toys that would occur over the next decades. (Kids also really liked the long, rumbly "Moo-oo-oo" of the cow.)

See 'n Say worked very much like a gramophone. The child pointed the arrow to the picture of the animal he or she wanted to hear and pulled the string. A needle engaged a disk on which sounds were recorded—very much like a small record—and the vibrations were projected through a plastic cone. The child heard ducks, dogs, frogs and more.

In later years, the pull-string would be replaced by a lever and the recorded disk by a computer chip. Mattel would expand the line to include licensed characters and more traditional learning activities. But what has never changed has been the excitement of children making things happen and at the same time discovering new things in their worlds.

1965
Tonka
Mighty Dump
Truck

As America emerged from World War II, the nation set about building for the future, and it was only natural that kids would respond eagerly to the toy versions of the cranes and steam shovels they saw all around them. In a time of building optimism, the sandbox was fertile ground for development and imagination.

Mound Metalcraft was founded in a schoolhouse basement in Mound, Minnesota, near Lake Minnetonka, which is where the name for the trucks would come from. Originally founded to produce metal garden supplies, the company also started making a line of toy vehicles. In its first year of operation, 1947, the company produced about 37,000 trucks in two styles: a crane (#150) and a steam shovel (#100). The toys were instant hits.

These were some tough toys, and they stood up to hard-playing kids. The company abandoned gardening, changed its name to Tonka and, literally, beat its plowshares into an ever-growing fleet of vehicles.

Kids loved Tonka trucks for the realism of the play and their virtual indestructibility. Can't play on the living room carpet with a truck covered in mud? Hose it down and it's ready to go.

Tonka continued to grow and expand, and nearly every boy since the baby boomer generation has a favorite Tonka truck and a favorite Tonka story. In 1965, Tonka introduced what would become its best-selling truck ever—the Tonka Mighty Dump Truck. This item would be Tonka's consistent best-seller throughout the rest of the century, and though Tonka toys would acquire electronics and characters, the basic imaginative play of trucks—building, rolling—would make the Tonka name synonymous with imagination.

"You knocked my block off!"

1966 Rock 'Em Sock 'Em Robots

A large part of a generation of kids grew up saying "He knocked my block off!" after the famous commercial for the Rock 'Em Sock 'Em Robots, where Junior handily dispatches Dad in the ring. In 1966, this was the coolest way imaginable to duke it out. Kids made the Marx toy with its two classic themes—boxing and robots—an instant hit. Squared off in the ring were the Blue Bomber and the Red Rocker, and neither bees nor butterflies figured in the boxing. Part of the fun was how basic and clunky the toy was. All kids had to do was use the handles to move the Bomber and the Rocker around the ring, throwing punches with a push of the button. Ultimately, amid the clash and clatter of plastic, one robot would land a punch on the other's chin and his head would ratchet up, ending the round. Push down on the head and start going again: Kids kept at it for hours.

Mattel acquired the rights and reintroduced the original version of the toy, which had been produced into the early 1970s, for the 2001 holidays. It was, unsurprisingly, a smash hit. Maybe the generation that grew up playing with the original wanted to prove that Dad's robot could throw a mean punch after all.

Kids made the Marx toy with its two classic themes an instant hit.

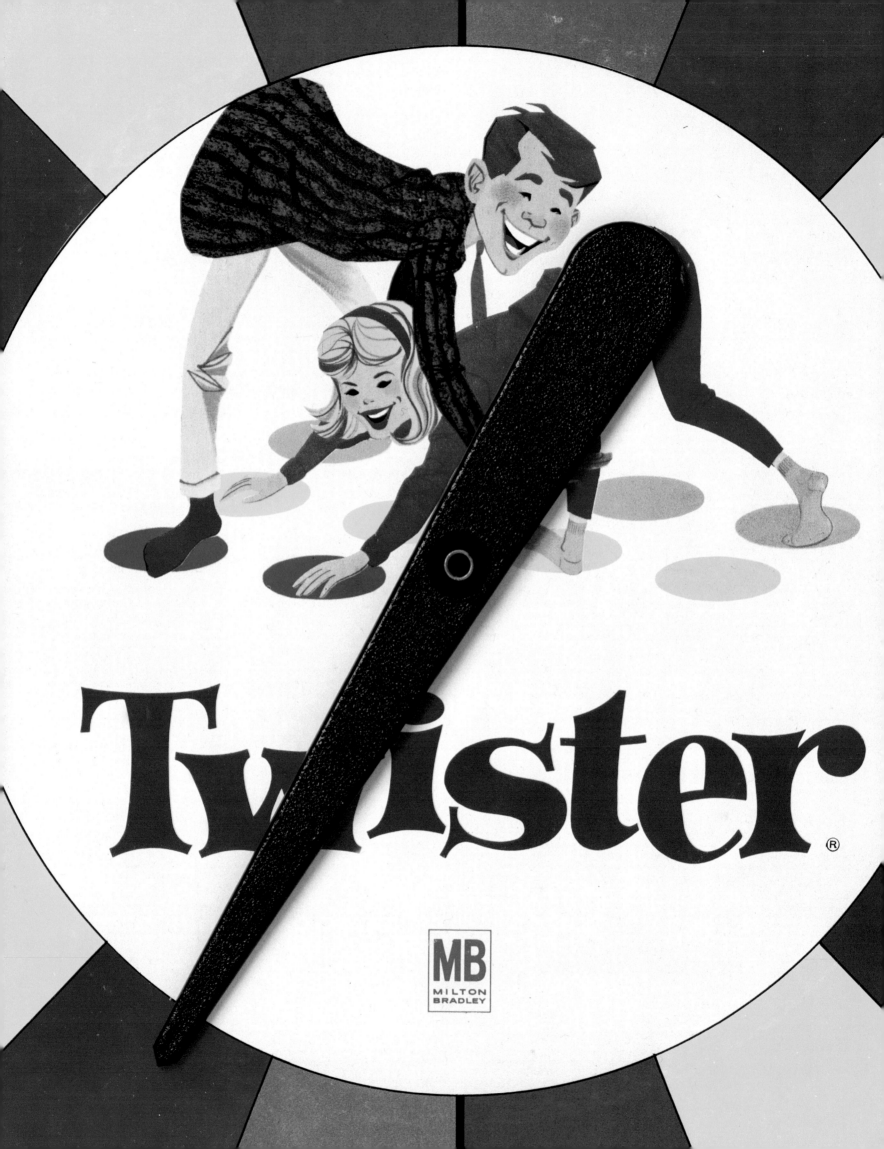

1966 Twister

It was the phenomenon that almost wasn't. How many millions of people have played Twister since it first hit the stores in 1966? Milton Bradley estimates that more than twenty million games have been sold since its introduction.

But as popular as the game is, it was just one day and one lucky break away from being an also-ran. On May 3, 1966, Milton Bradley got the news that Sears was canceling its order, saying the game wasn't appropriate for kids. Evidently, the PR folks didn't get the news. That night they took the game to Johnny Carson, and he played it with Eva Gabor. People could really see just how much fun Twister was.

The next morning, there was a line about fifty people deep in front of Abercrombie & Fitch in New York wanting the game. Twister had found an audience.

1967
Spirograph

Imagine, if you will, op art meets mathematics with a little bit of the psychedelic thrown in. That was Spirograph, a simple but amazingly well-engineered collection of plastic gears and oblongs with holes in them. When they were put together, and a ballpoint pen was put through one of the holes, the gears turned around one another with the pen tracing the path, and the result was amazing geometric designs. When all the pieces were set just right, even the most abandoned scribbler was able to create intricate designs in a multitude of colors. (The toy came with red, blue and black pens.)

Designed and marketed by Denys Fisher in 1965, the toy really took off. All of a sudden kids could envision themselves as accomplished artists with very little effort, and the toy became one of the biggest sellers of 1967.

There was something about the designs that caught the spirit of the times: the influence of colorful fashion, rock and roll and a fascination with geometric design. Even the color palette was soon "liberated" to reflect the new tastes of the times—kids were thrilled to find aqua or char-treuse pens for making their Spirographics in the stationery departments of local stores.

There was something irrepressibly mod about the drawings, but at the same time they had a touch of science just right for a country that was about to put a man on the Moon.

Anyone could now create intricate designs in a multitude of colors.

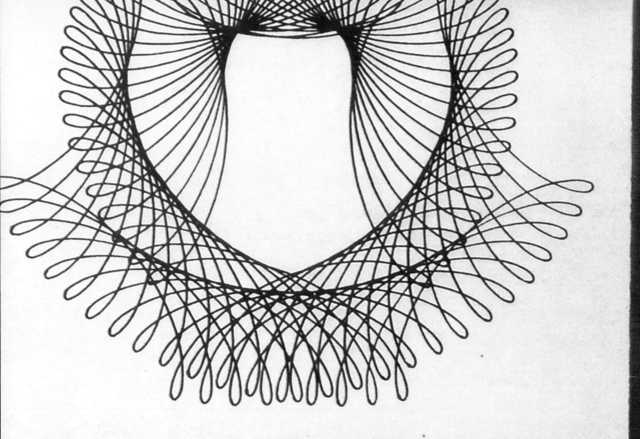

HOW TO DRAW WITH
SPIROGRAPH

1968 Hot Wheels Cars

No miniature car had ever given kids such an exhilarating sense of excitement and speed. Today, Hot Wheels is still the top-selling toy brand in the U.S.

For Elliot Handler, one of the founders of Mattel, Hot Wheels cars were a special—and important—project. In 1968, the die-cast car business was big and growing, but the vast majority of the cars were replicas, and the play was, perhaps, a little calm for boys who liked action.

Handler knew that what boys wanted in their cars was speed, speed and more speed. Throw in a few daring stunts and that death-defying leap from the kitchen table to the countertop, and it was die-cast heaven.

Instead of wheels attached directly to the body of the car, as in most die-cast toys at the time, Handler added an axle and plastic wheels and created cars that could really rock out. Handler was also very hands-on in the design process and could often be found deeply involved in projects right alongside the designers and engineers.

In 1968, the very first Hot Wheels car rolled off the production line. It was the Custom Camaro, and it was significant not just because it represented the beginning of the Hot Wheels brand but because consumers would see the car first in miniature before G.M. had unveiled the real thing. Mattel then introduced its track system for Hot Wheels cars, and for the growing number of fans, this was the best yet. Complete with launchers like the Power Booster, which used foam wheels to shoot the cars along the track, Hot Wheels cars quickly outpaced the competition and became the cool die-cast cars that kids had to have.

Like many other toys of the period, Hot Wheels cars had their own animated TV series, which followed the adventures of teenage race-car drivers in the "Hot Wheels Club," a time-tested plotline for younger kids.

Since 1968, Mattel has sold more than two billion cars. The line has expanded to include high-end collectibles, NASCAR licenses and countless play sets. Hot Wheels was the top-selling toy brand in the United States for the last years of the 1990s and the first years of the new century, proving conclusively that the need for speed, the fantasy of racing and the really cool look of Hot Wheels cars is something kids will always love.

1968
Lite Brite

The late 1960s was an incredible time for what were then relatively high-tech arts-and-crafts toys. Kids momentarily put down their crayons to indulge in new kinds of creativity.

Lite-Brite was definitely one of the coolest toys ever. To this day, countless adults can still sing the commercial jingle:
"Lite-Brite,
Making things with light,
What a sight,
Making things with Lite-Brite."

In 1968, and for many years afterward, the toy topped many children's wish lists, and many adults who were kids when Lite-Brite came out vividly remember having—or wanting—their own Lite-Brite.

The unit came with black construction paper sheets with preprinted pictures, as well as blank sheets for kids who wanted to be completely free to design. Plus, it had more than three hundred different colored pegs that went into the holes.

To create with Lite-Brite, kids put the sheet on the unit, plugged in the pegs and switched it on. That was the moment they waited for—when their works of art would light up in full color.

Refill kits were made with many different licenses, and Lite-Brite has never been out of production since it was first introduced. And while perhaps only a handful of the legions of kids who created with Lite-Brite have gone on to become artists, at least one, Steve de Frank, has. This artist has used Lite-Brite as the basis for creations on a grand scale, elevating those little crafty pegs to a legitimate, mainstream art form.

1969 Nerf

The world's first indoor ball!

What do most of the popular and enduring toys have in common? They broke rules. And one of the biggest rule-breakers of all time was the Nerf ball. After all, what mom was going to allow her kids to play with a ball in the house?

Well, Nerf certainly broke that rule. Suddenly you could play basketball, soccer, even football indoors—without breaking anything. Score one for kids, and score one for mom.

Of course, as Nerf inventor Reyn Guyer says, "For every great idea, there are usually, oh, several hundred rotten ideas." In 1969, Guyer and his designers were trying to develop a caveman game. It was like Twister, which was a huge hit for Guyer in 1966, in that the people playing became an integral part of the game. To keep people from stepping on specific squares, the designers cut up pieces of black foam. As part of this game, players had to throw the foam at one another.

The game was getting nowhere, Guyer notes, but one of the designers started just throwing the foam. Now that was fun! And the rest is an international toy industry phenomenon.

Though Nerf started with just a single ball, the line developed over the years to include almost every kind of ball imaginable.

Nerf became a classic staple brand—the perfect response to every mom who's ever said, "Outdoors with that!" And Guyer says that every Christmas someone throws one of the original pieces of Nerf foam at his Christmas tree—as a way of commemorating how a bad idea turned into a bonanza.

1973

1982

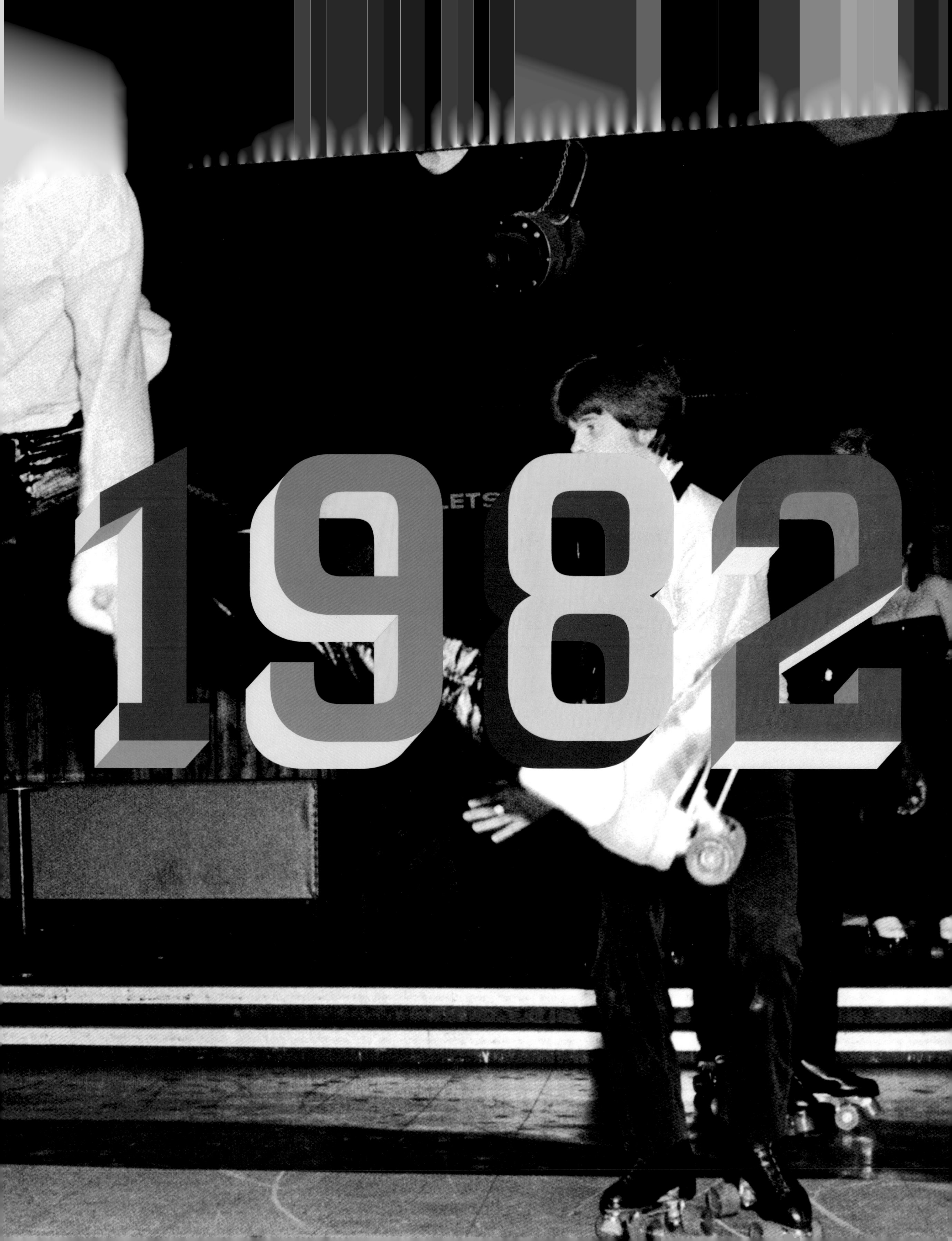

John Travolta and Karen Gorney, *Saturday Night Fever*, 1977

By 1972, the revolution of the 1960s had finally arrived in the mainstream and its impact on popular culture was profound. The bright colors, longer hairstyles and relaxed attitudes that had symbolized the counterculture were now seen everywhere. TV shows like "The Brady Bunch" would redefine the notion of the family—worlds away from the staid shows of the 1950s. ■ Kids' television was particularly dominant, with Saturday mornings devoted to such cartoons as "Scooby Doo," "Fat Albert" and the "Cosby Kids," the most popular shows of the decade. Adults spent their evenings watching "Mary Tyler Moore," "M*A*S*H," "The Waltons" and "Columbo."

Daytime was dominated by a new generation of soaps appealing to younger viewers, particularly college students, who made cult hits out of "All My Children" and "The Young and the Restless," and Phil Donahue opened the door to all the talk shows that would follow in the '80s and '90s. ■ Traditional taboos disappeared, and shows like "All in the Family," "Maude" and "the Jeffersons," where sensitive topics were treated with warmth and humor, and "Saturday Night

Bicentennial stamp, 1976

Live" pushed the limits of the subjects and situations people would accept on TV, and even what constituted comedy. Not since "Laugh-In," a decade earlier, had shows so specifically defined what was funny. ■ During the '60s and early '70s, television had kept movie audiences home, but by the middle of the decade movies were back in force. The '70s saw the beginning of the blockbuster movie with *Jaws* and *The Exorcist*. Dolby sound and advances in special effects made possible such films as *Star Wars*, which would establish the market for movie-relat-

ed toys. Nostalgia for the '50s and early '60s inspired *American Graffiti* and the Broadway hit *Grease*. But it would be *Saturday Night Fever* with John Travolta that would establish disco as the trend in music and fashion for the late '70s. ■ Music was eclectic, encompassing all kinds of rock, country and, ultimately, disco. There was no one sound that defined the era, so Aerosmith and the Bee Gees, Led Zeppelin and Billy Joel, the Carpenters and Bruce Springsteen all had legions of loyal fans. They could now be played in cars as well, as 8-tracks and the cassette recorder made music more portable than it had ever been. ■ It was a huge decade for toys, which ran the gamut from the cuteness

1973-1982
The Reign of Pop Culture

Star Wars movie poster, 1977

of Holly Hobbie to the intensity of Dungeons & Dragons. The Uno card game made its debut, and Othello brought back the strategy game. The Six Million Dollar Man was one of the top-selling action figures, along with a restaged G.I. Joe, and *Star Wars* would close the decade, redefining action figures forever. Mattel's Handheld Football Game introduced the handheld

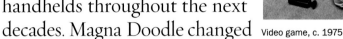

electronic game and was the forerunner of many successful handhelds throughout the next decades. Magna Doodle changed

Video game, c. 1975

drawing toys with its magnetic stylus and magical erase feature, and would become the best-selling design toy of all time. Preschoolers loved Weebles, Major Morgan and Alphie, and the entire nation went wild for a very puzzling cube created by Erno Rubik. ■ For all the entertainment, these were challenging times as well. The U.S. finally withdrew

The cast of "Mary Tyler Moore," 1977

from Vietnam, after years of protests, and it was the first time that America had not been triumphant in an overseas war. Veterans were not heroes, and the lack of

Pet Rock, 1975

resolution would haunt the country for the rest of the century. There were advances in civil rights and the women's movement, but there was still far to go as the new and old ways continued to clash. ■ The Arab oil embargo caused severe shortages in the U.S. Prices went through the roof, and long lines at gas stations and gas rationing were common. The Watergate break-in

"Charlie's Angels," 1978

would topple President Nixon, and no matter how cheerful "The Partridge Family" was, the economy fell into a severe recession. ■ Yet, despite this, the culture remained upbeat, spurred in part by the huge celebrations of the Bicentennial in 1976, as well as major advances in space exploration, with the U.S. and the U.S.S.R. working together for the first time. ■ The baby boomers were growing up, and as they had for years, were dictating the trajectory of the

Scooby-Doo and Shaggy, 1980s

culture. The "hippie freaks" of the 1960s were now mainstream consumers, and their tastes and interests would continue to drive consumption patterns. Though they had rebelled against the establishment as defined by their parents in the 1960s, a decade later they were increasingly defining the establishment that would lead the nation into the '80s.

1973
Baby Alive

Interacting with what seems like a real baby or a real playmate has remained an unchanging and essential form of play for decades.

Beginning in the 1950s—the heyday of the mass-market baby doll—every holiday season brought a new amazing baby that promised to make doll-play better than it ever had been before. What was remarkable about these dolls was that the relatively simple (at least by twenty-first century standards) mechanisms were all but invisible. The list of these dolls reads like a Who's Who of dolls over the latter part of the twentieth century, and includes classics that are still delighting little girls—Betsy Wetsy, Tiny Tears, Thumbelina, Patty Play Pal and many more.

In 1973, Kenner launched Baby Alive. Like the other dolls, she was a cute, hard-plastic baby doll. However, there may have been drink-and-wet dolls before, but there had never been an eat-and- . . . well, you get the idea: Little girls fed Baby Alive what looked like real baby food—the strained kind. And in a little while, thanks to an internal mechanism, the inevitable happened, and Baby Alive would require a diaper change. She also moved and made baby sounds, so little

girls got a pretty complete pretend mommy experience. Though this level of reality was considered controversial by some, little girls loved the doll. Baby Alive became the top-selling doll of the year. In 1990, Kenner reintroduced Baby Alive, and she was just as popular as she had been the first time around, selling some nine million dolls.

Feature dolls remain major sellers every year, and thanks to new, more sophisticated and less expensive technology, they now do more than ever before. But the activity they encourage—interacting with what seems like a real baby or a real playmate—has remained an unchanging and essential form of play for decades.

1975
The Tuneyville
Choo-Choo

At the beginning of the 1980s, technology was beginning to show up in more and more toys—particularly in the preschool categories. In those days before the computer chip, the technological magic was mechanical rather than digital. Wind-ups of all sorts were hugely popular, and toys that did things seemingly on their own caught the imaginations of toy buyers and children alike.

One of the leaders in this type of innovation was Tomy Corporation. With its Tuneyville Choo-Choo, first introduced in 1975, it created a sensation that would last for many years, with more than three million toys sold worldwide. What's remarkable about the toy is that as innovative as it was, it worked much the same way as music boxes or player pianos of a century earlier.

When kids dropped one of the plastic disks into the top of the train, raised bumps on the record would trigger electronic music sensors in a specific pattern (just as music boxes of the nineteenth century used spools with raised spindles to play precisely tuned metal keys) that would play one of eleven different songs—about three to a disk. As it played music, the train would roll along, and kids were enchanted because, to them, it was completely magical.

This introduction of the Tuneyville Choo-Choo was just one of the significant breakthroughs Tomy had achieved over the years. In 1956, the company launched one of the first battery-operated toys, the Bubble Blowing Elephant. In 1964 it launched a new voice mechanism that would replace the type commonly in use, revolutionizing talking toys.

Throughout the 1980s, technological developments would continue to inspire toy designers, and chips would be used in addition to these mechanical devices (the Tuneyville Choo-Choo is still manufactured today), with Tomy remaining at the forefront of innovation and technology. Yet no matter how it happened, for kids, the magic of one's toys seeming to come to life would remain a key element of preschool play and would redefine how they related to and interacted with their toys.

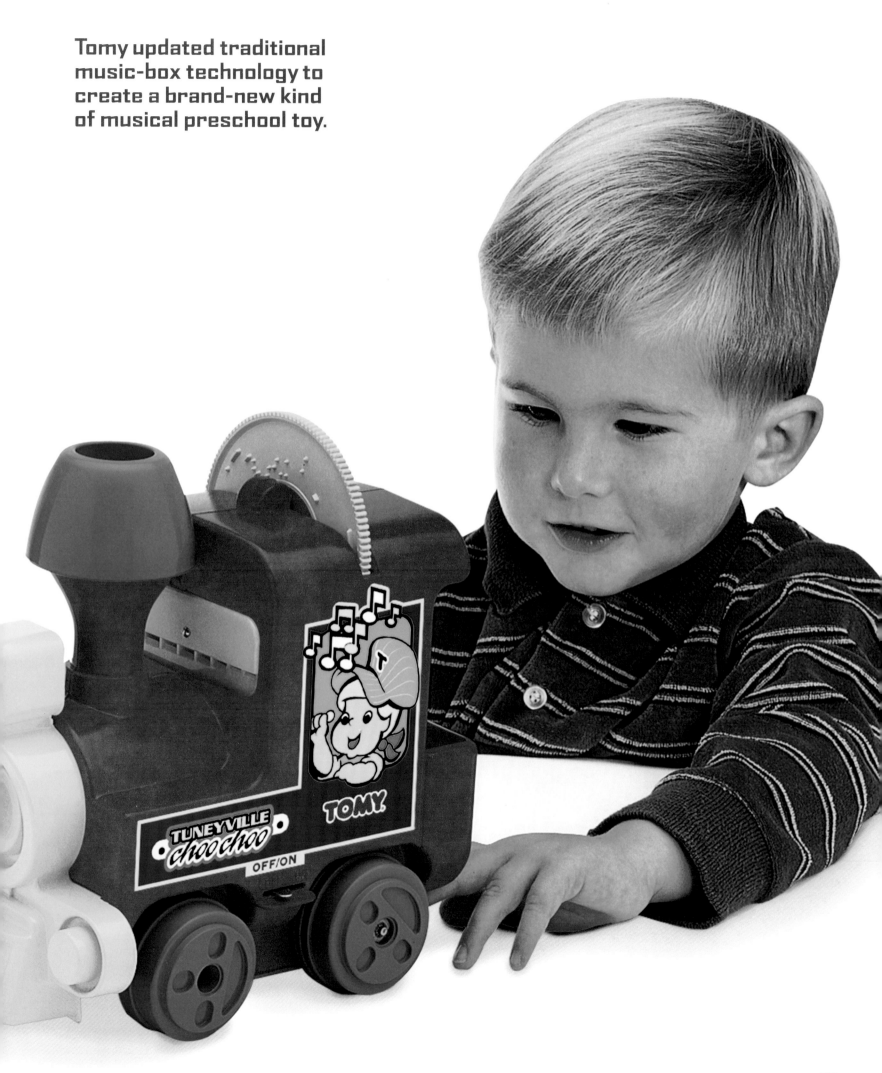

Tomy updated traditional music-box technology to create a brand-new kind of musical preschool toy.

TUNEYVILLE choochoo

OFF/ON

TOMY

1976
Stretch Armstrong

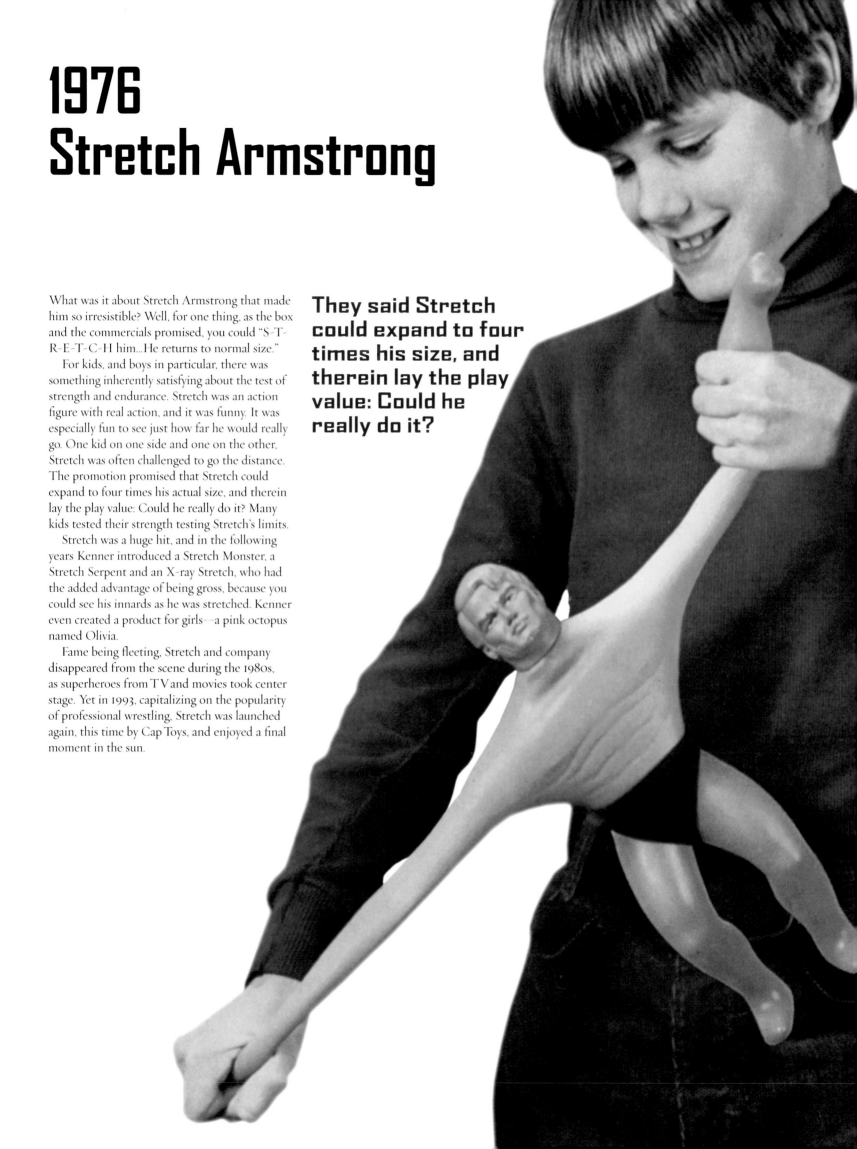

What was it about Stretch Armstrong that made him so irresistible? Well, for one thing, as the box and the commercials promised, you could "S-T-R-E-T-C-H him...He returns to normal size."

For kids, and boys in particular, there was something inherently satisfying about the test of strength and endurance. Stretch was an action figure with real action, and it was funny. It was especially fun to see just how far he would really go. One kid on one side and one on the other, Stretch was often challenged to go the distance. The promotion promised that Stretch could expand to four times his actual size, and therein lay the play value: Could he really do it? Many kids tested their strength testing Stretch's limits.

Stretch was a huge hit, and in the following years Kenner introduced a Stretch Monster, a Stretch Serpent and an X-ray Stretch, who had the added advantage of being gross, because you could see his innards as he was stretched. Kenner even created a product for girls—a pink octopus named Olivia.

Fame being fleeting, Stretch and company disappeared from the scene during the 1980s, as superheroes from TV and movies took center stage. Yet in 1993, capitalizing on the popularity of professional wrestling, Stretch was launched again, this time by Cap Toys, and enjoyed a final moment in the sun.

They said Stretch could expand to four times his size, and therein lay the play value: Could he really do it?

1977 Star Wars

There was plenty of action and excitement, but there was also something powerful in the message of using "the Force."

With *Star Wars* having been such a dominant force in the toy industry for more than a quarter of a century by 2003, it's easy to forget that when it was released in 1977, the original movie (*Episode IV: A New Hope*, for those really in the know) was actually nothing more than a Western in space. At the time, George Lucas was not an auteur—he was a guy making movies. If this one made money, he had plans for a sequel, or two.

Yet *Star Wars* affected the culture in ways that no movie since has been able to replicate. In an increasingly cynical time, the simple message of "the Force"—along with plenty of action—resonated powerfully. It provided fodder for the imagination, and was the beginning of a global franchise in toys.

Kenner hadn't anticipated how huge the original movie would be. They introduced puzzles, games and other fast-to-market products, but it would be holiday 1977 before action figures hit the stores. No matter, demand was still huge. It was the following year that Kenner ramped up production. Joining the initial line, Luke, Princess Leia, R2-D2 and Chewbacca, were all the lead characters. With the next two movies, more toys would be sold, and many adults who grew up during the peak *Star Wars* toys years recall fondly that every Christmas and birthday brought more *Star Wars* toys.

With millions of toys and dollars made, *Star Wars* also transformed action figures and movie licensing. Whereas BSW (before *Star Wars*) movie toys were a small part of the overall marketing and merchandising of movies, ASW (after *Star Wars*) toy development began almost as soon as scripts were green-lighted or even in pitch meetings.

Star Wars proved that toys could become a lifelong hobby. No movie or toy line has ever inspired the level of passion—obsession?—that *Star Wars* has. In 2003, more than half a million Web sites are devoted at least in part to *Star Wars* toys. Collectors go to conventions, wait hours at toy stores for new releases, happily pay huge sums for rare figures and flood the Internet with discussions about characters and plot points.

Star Wars also created the mass-market collectibles market. Toys weren't just for kids anymore, and manufacturers would respond, creating collectible versions of virtually every kind of toy. Advances in design technology and manufacturing, meant increasingly fine detail, character replication and play value. By the end of the twentieth century, even a three-inch action figure would have some kind of "magical" element that would further bring the world of *Star Wars* alive for its legions of fans.

Star Wars introduced the world to the Force, and it introduced the toy industry to the economic force of consumers (children and adults) who eagerly sought to express their connection to a story and its characters through toys. In the years after *Star Wars*, the market would be flooded with action figures and play sets. The action figure as lifestyle product was here to stay.

It took its name from the classic game Simon Says, but in 1978, Milton Bradley's Simon introduced a new kind of electronic game that swept the nation. Developer Ralph Baer created the game after an early version designed for the first Atari systems. He reconfigured it, adding tones to the colors, and Milton Bradley launched the game in 1978.

It was, and still is, a huge hit. There is something classic and competitive about the game-play. Its simplicity is part of the secret: Follow the pattern of lights and sounds until you forget, and it's the next person's turn.

Simple...or not—one of Simon's main contributions to the toy industry was to get families playing games again. Simon also helped establish the electronic board-game sector of the industry, and would inspire many offspring—including Super Simon, which allowed head-to-head competition, and Pocket Simon, for play on the go.

In 1999, in the tradition of Simon, Milton Bradley launched Bop-It, followed by Bop-It Extreme—all building on the same play pattern, and all of which have been successful. After all, it's fun to have your toys boss you around.

Simple...or not— Simon got families playing games again.

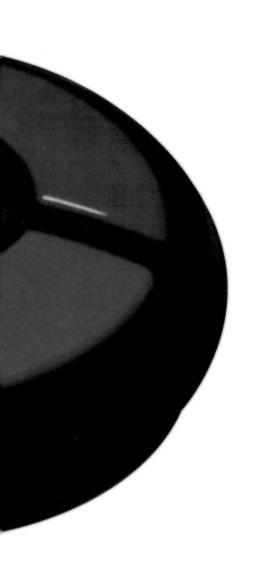

1979 Strawberry Shortcake

Strawberry and her friends smelled of fruit, candy or flowers. Along with other characters of the time, she created a new era of sweetness.

The late 1970s saw a proliferation of cute characters. Starting with Holly Hobbie in the early part of the decade and inspired partially by the work of earlier artist-authors like Joan Walsh Anglund (*A Friend Is a Very Special Person*), there was a whole cute movement sweeping the country. Some even trace the advent of cute to the sad-eyed kids painted by Margaret and Walter Keane, which were huge in the early years of the decade. Wherever it came from, by the mid-1970s adorable was definitely in.

Greeting-card giant American Greetings and its affiliated company, Those Characters from Cleveland, had staked a claim to this design trend, and in the late 1970s, they introduced the little girl (and friends) who would represent the pinnacle of cute for the next several years—Strawberry Shortcake.

The five-and-a-half-inch dolls, which Kenner unveiled in 1979, weren't merely more cute faces. They smelled really good. Advances in plastic technology meant that the fragrance could be integrated into the doll—and it would last. And Strawberry wasn't alone. The initial line also included Lemon Meringue, Huckleberry Pie, Raspberry Tart and Orange Blossom, along with that nasty guy from down the lane, the Purple Pieman. Over twenty-five million dolls and more than thirty-five million accessories were sold during the height of Strawberry fever.

The success of Strawberry Shortcake was such that it inspired all kinds of similar products—Herself the Elf, Peppermint Rose, Rose Petal Place and so forth. But none of them could ever equal the appeal of Strawberry and her friends.

Collectors have kept the dolls alive, and in 2003, Bandai will be reintroducing the line to the mass market—this time for the generation of girls whose mothers remember the originals and their intoxicating fruit fragrances.

Kids love to drive. In fact, driving is one of the top role-playing activities, right up there with talking on the telephone. Yeah, it's cool to have a little steering wheel on your car seat or high chair. But that first set of real wheels that you gave you mobility, well, that wasn't just a toy—that was a rite of passage.

Of course, kids had been mobile for years. Bikes, trikes, pedal cars and even the famous Big Wheel had kept them mobile, to say nothing of building their quadriceps. But in 1979, Little Tikes introduced something completely new, a car that seemed realistic, and that was ideal for kids as young as eighteen months old.

Open the door, get behind the wheel, put the pedal to the metal...Okay, no pedal, and no metal. Put your feet to the floor, and you're cruising. It wasn't about speed; it was about being in the driver's seat.

The Cozy Coupe proved so popular that it became America's best-selling car model, even counting grown-up cars. Since its introduction, it's won all kinds of awards, and in 2000, like any popular car that's been around for a while, it got a whole new look.

1979 Cozy Coupe

1980
Rubik's Cube

The interior mechanism of the Rubik's Cube is one of the engineering marvels of twentieth-century toy design.

Manipulative puzzles have been around for centuries. In ancient China, puzzlers wrestled with solving pyramid-shaped tangrams. Wooden puzzles were popular in the nineteenth and early twentieth centuries, and even in plastics, such 1960s introductions as the Soma Cube and Instant Insanity had each enjoyed a brief popularity.

Yet all of these together were nothing to the global phenomenon set off by Rubik's Cube. The three-by-three-by-three cube was created by Hungarian Erno Rubik in 1974, and it was the first manipulative puzzle that stayed in one integrated piece while it was being manipulated. In fact, the interior mechanism of the Rubik's Cube (go ahead and look—you've always wanted an excuse to break it anyway) is one of the engineering marvels of twentieth-century toy design.

After three years of effort in collaboration with a local manufacturing company, Rubik finally got his cube on the shelf in 1977. Sales were slow but steady throughout 1978, but nothing to indicate what was to come. In fact, the cube might have stayed behind the Iron Curtain had it not been noticed by Dr. Tibor Laczi, who "discovered" it on a trip to Budapest and took it to the Nuremberg, Germany, toy show in 1979. He found no distributors, but he did meet Tom Kremer, a toy inventor with a company called Seven Towns, who would bring the cube to the U.S. and sign a licensing agreement with Ideal. The cube was officially unveiled in the U.S. at the Toy Fair in 1980.

By this time, interest was growing around the world, and the infectious fun of handling the cube, not to mention the frustration of trying to get all six sides back in order, was building steadily. In 1980, the cube sold a million pieces or more. In each successive year, the number grew exponentially, and when Ideal was acquired by CBS, the cube had become an international sensation.

It had been front-page news, had been on every conceivable TV show, had been used as a prop in movies...you name it. There were nearly seventy books written on the cube and solving it, its name had become an adjective in dictionaries, and it had even become a Saturday morning superhero in "Rubik the Amazing Cube."

This astonishing level of success was also an international headache, as counterfeit cubes started appearing on the market everywhere. Although the name was protected, the mechanism that made it all work was patented only in Hungary, so many companies introduced cubist puzzles. Ultimately, the market was flooded, and in 1984, the market for the cubes collapsed.

Kremer, however, was not going to give up. He bought back the rights and slowly started to reintroduce the cube. In 1995, OddzOn relaunched it and a whole line of Rubik's puzzles. People started playing with it again. Phil Donahue tried to solve a $1 million gold cube inset with precious gems. A new generation discovered the challenges. No matter how the toy market twists and turns, it seems the cube is here to stay.

In the early '80s, playgrounds and backyards rang with the cries of children invoking "the Power of Grayskull." He-Man and the Masters of the Universe offered the ultimate fantasy for kids—virtually unstoppable power. As the play went, even the most mild-mannered kid could be transformed into a superhero by invoking this mythic power, and kids around the world bought into the stories of Prince Adam, who transformed into the impressively muscled He-Man to battle villainy.

While the basic story line was nothing new, drawn as it was from years of similar successes and even Greek mythology, it was brand new to the kids of the time, who made the TV show (which premiered in 1983) and the related toy line two of the biggest hits of the decade. In 2003, adults who remember hours spent watching TV and playing with the Masters toys can still recount complete episodes.

And what toys they were. After years of relatively static action figures (excepting, of course, G.I. Joe's Kung Fu Grip), Mattel introduced figures with the "Power Punch." Twist the He-Man figure at the waist, and he could deliver a rubber-band-driven right hook to the evil Skeletor. (Presumably He-Man took his licks in return, as Skeletor was similarly equipped.)

The early 1980s was also the heyday of the play set—large environments in which stories came to life—and the ultimate prize of the period, according to adults who remember getting it (or not), was Castle Grayskull, complete with working elevator, drawbridge and trapdoor. In 1985, Princess Adora, Adam's sister, took the stage as She-Ra Princess of Power. Wonder Woman helped pave the way in the late '70s, but She-Ra was one of the first female heroes embraced by boys and girls alike.

Given the power and popularity of the show, it was not surprising that Tom Wolfe borrowed the phrase "Masters of the Universe" for his 1987 satire *The Bonfire of the Vanities*. In all likelihood, just a few years before he took on Wall Street, the character Sherman McCoy may himself have been invoking the Power of Grayskull in play.

In 2002, Mattel staged a major relaunch of the brand—banking once more on the power of a now-classic and indomitable superhero.

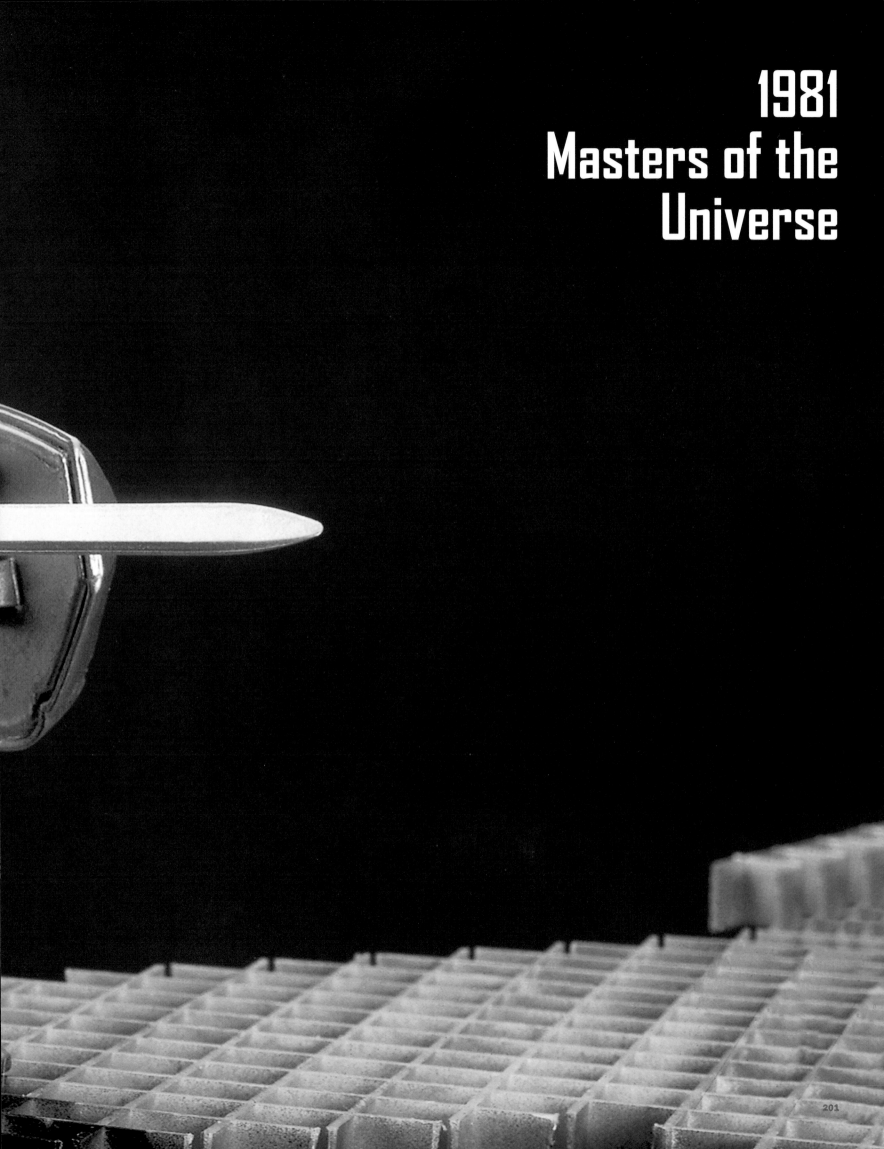

1981
Masters of the
Universe

Horses. Hair play. Fashion. Colors. Glitter. Collectibles. Put any two of these together and you may have a concept for a girls' toy. Put them all together and you've got a virtually guaranteed hit. That's exactly what Hasbro did in the early 1980s with the introduction of the My Little Pony line. Its success gave an entirely new meaning to the concept of a stable brand.

Of course, girls had loved horses for years. Movies like *National Velvet* and *My Friend Flicka* are classics, and literature for young girls is full of horse stories. The Barbie doll had a horse, and there were all kinds of collectible horses for play and display.

But what set My Little Pony apart was that it wasn't just a horse for a girl to love, it was a whole world of horses where there were no humans allowed, except for the millions of little girls who loved them, played with them and took care of their flowing manes.

Hasbro's first line of six soft vinyl horses in 1982 included Blue Belle, Blossom, Butterscotch, Cotton Candy, Minty and Snuzzle. Each of the horses was unique, with an individual marking on her hindquarters. What's more, each pony had a lever under its chin that allowed it to swish its tail and move its ears.

For the next few years, My Little Pony was win, place and show with little girls. My Little Pony inspired a movie, a TV show and, according to women who were little girls at the time, a real passion for ponies and pony paraphernalia. For the next ten years, the line kept growing, and soon My Little Pony came in a variety of shapes and sizes—unicorns, flying horses, princesses, brides, baby ponies, rainbow ponies and so forth—and each had a magical, whimsical name. The prevailing logic was that if it could be a little girl's fantasy, it could be a pony. And it worked.

It was a whole world of horses where there were no humans allowed, except for the millions of little girls who loved them.

1982 My Little Pony

1982 Trivial Pursuit

Wouldn't it be great if an argument you had with a friend ended up making you both multi-millionaires?

Well, that's exactly what happened to Scott Abbott, a sports editor with *The Canadian Press*, and Chris Haney, photo editor for the *Montreal Gazette*. They argued over who was the better game player and—as with most boys' play—the argument turned into a contest to see who had a better grasp of trivial information.

What happened next, though, was anything but trivial. They produced the game, which had an innovative folding board, a square box and pieces that were very expensive, at least for the toy industry. Moreover, it was priced at almost $35, breaking the previous price ceiling for games. Even if the price wasn't too high, conventional wisdom had it that adults didn't play games. And who would ever make room on a shelf for a box that shape? At the end of the Toy Fair in 1982, it seemed as though there might be a market for a few games at specialty stores, but that would be about it.

Then Linda Pezzano took over. An innovative marketer with a flair for the nontraditional, she was a perfect person for the job—the challenge of getting adults to play a game that tested their grasp of often arcane information. Pezzano sent games to every celebrity mentioned in the game, hosted parties for the media at her house and gave away sample cards to just about anyone who would look at them. Over the next year, the tsunami of publicity made the game not just a household word, but a must-have. At a time when game manufacturers considered 100,000 games sold a major hit, Trivial Pursuit sold millions. By its twentieth anniversary, sales of the game, now licensed by Milton Bradley, had surpassed 70 million copies in 17 countries and 26 languages.

Most important, the success of Trivial Pursuit created the adult board-game category and revolutionized game design and marketing.

Not a bad way to settle a score between friends.

An argument made two friends multimillionaires—and also made toy history.

The original Trivial Pursuit board, made on December 16, 1979, by Scott Abbott and Chris Haney, the day after they created the game

1983 Care Bears

The initial press release introduced them as "Roly-poly little bears who live high in a land of rainbows and fluffy clouds called 'Care-a-lot.'"

1992

The baby boomers were finally raking it in, and they were spending it—on themselves and their kids. Houses and cars became bigger and two-income families were the norm. As a result, kids' lives became much more organized, and the soccer mom in the minivan became one of the icons of the decade. ■ When kids weren't being shuttled to and from after-school activities, they were tuning into new cable channels like MTV and pestering their parents to buy them one of those new compact disc players. Not since the 1920s had there been so many excesses, and Tom Wolfe satirized it all in *The Bonfire of the Vanities.* Even the 1987 stock market crash couldn't dampen the spirit of having more, having better, and with a little luck having it all. ■ Fashion was all about name brands, and labels from designers such as Ralph Lauren, Perry Ellis and Calvin Klein started

Madonna, 1983

appearing on the outside of garments where they could be seen to best advantage. Preppies were hot for a while. Movie and TV stars redefined over-the-top elegance, and the decade even saw its own fairy-tale wedding—the ultimate fantasy—as Diana Spencer became the Princess of Wales. ■ All of this excess very nearly distracted us from the serious issues of the day. Reagan had declared war on drugs and condemned the "evil empire," but the cold war would end and the Berlin Wall would tumble. ■ It was a time of upheaval in the social structure as well. The construction of the family was changing, and the concept of the "blended" or "extended" family began to reshape relationships. ■ And still, popular culture was a dominant force. ■ In music, Madonna was both a fashion plate and a star, Cyndi Lauper just wanted to have fun and Culture Club, the Bangles and Duran Duran led the new wave. Punk and rock exploded with new groups

1983-1992
Affluence
and the "Me"
Decade

arriving almost daily, driven in large part by MTV. What a group looked like became as important as how it sounded. The big development of the decade, though, was the rise of rap music. It provided a new sound and a new politics that shook the music industry out of its complacency. And more than twenty years after they first hit the United States, the Rolling Stones were still touring...as were the Grateful Dead. ■ On television, there was

Pac-Man video game, 1980s

Run DMC, 1987

a new edge that seemed to reflect the time and the changing structure of the family. Mom could talk back, as in "Roseanne." Or she could be a successful, savvy woman, as in "the Cosby Show." Aaron Spelling would dominate the airwaves with prime-time soaps such as "Dallas," "Knots's Landing," "Falcon Crest" and "Dynasty." These in turn would inspire fashion and promote the idea that richer is better. ■ We were also ready to spill our guts on shows with one-name stars—Oprah, Sally, Geraldo, Jerry. It was the beginning of what would be called "reality" television in the next decade, and Andy Warhol's prediction a decade earlier that everyone would be famous for fifteen minutes didn't seem so farfetched. ■ In short, TV began

Cyndi Lauper, 1984

"Dallas," broadcast from 1978-1991

to dominate popular culture, and according to *TV Guide*, eighty-two percent of American adults watched TV for more than seven hours every day. Cable began to explode, and by the end of the decade, cable penetration would reach an all-time high. ■ The movies of the decade included *ET*, *The Big Chill* (perfect for boomers turning forty), *Back to the Future*, *Raiders of the Lost Ark*—a balance between the serious and the silly, as usual. ■ For toys, licensed merchandise became big business. Nearly every TV show for kids had a line of related products, and affluent consumers bought virtually all of them. After all, if one Smurf was good, a platoon was "awesome." Gobots and Koosh Balls and Micro Machines and Ninja Turtles were all huge hits. Cabbage Patch ushered in the decade of the must-have toy, and the Barbie doll (even pushing thirty) was hotter than ever. New technology was showing up in toys, which could do more than ever before. A new emphasis on educational toys helped kids reinforce

Punk fashion, 1985

traditional skills while preparing them for the world of computers. ■ It was, as every decade had been before, rife with contradictions:

The Big Chill movie poster, 1983

The advance of technology was tempered by the explosion of the Space Shuttle and intelligent political debate was tempered by the celebration of the less than intellectual Valley Girl. It was business as usual in the U.S.

1983 Care Bears

What was it about the '80s that inspired so much sweetness? Strawberry Shortcake was just finishing her first run in 1983 when Kenner launched its Care Bears line. The initial press release introduced them as "Roly-poly little bears who live high in a land of rainbows and fluffy clouds called 'Care-a-lot.' The bears regularly come to earth to make humans feel better and to help them share their feelings with others."

Their sweetness struck a chord, and the U.S.—and the world—went mad for the Care Bears. In the touchy-feely world of the '80s, when adults congregated to "share" their feelings and children were encouraged to be in touch with their emotions, Care Bears were a mass-market phenomenon that touched people of all ages. There was practically a bear for every occasion you could think of—and they came in all colors of the rainbow. And in the very '80s spirit of gender neutrality, the Care Bears appealed to many boys as well. Hey, everyone can use a hug sometimes.

Kenner would continue to release more Care Bears, including specific bears for special occasions—kind of like greeting cards—and would launch one of the most successful character licensing programs of all time. In other words, Care Bears were everywhere, and for a time, their loyal fans couldn't get enough.

The Care Bears starred in two full-length movies and their own TV show, which kept kids and adults involved in the brand. The original toys are now prized collectibles (many of them having been loved to tatters), and the line was recently reintroduced to a new crop of kids by Play Along.

1983 Cabbage Patch Kids

They began innocently enough, as these things often do. As the story went, they came from the cabbage patch, each one was individual and kids didn't own them, they adopted them. In 1976, artist Xavier Roberts created the dolls, called Little People, out of cloth and sold them at craft fairs to pay his college tuition. When arts-and-crafts—and the dolls very unusual look—became popular in 1980, he started a full-fledged manufacturing facility in a refurbished medical office in Cleveland, Georgia, aptly named Babyland General Hospital. There, children could see their dolls being "born" right out of a cabbage.

As awareness of the dolls and how they were born started appearing as a curiosity in media around the U.S., demand grew. Coleco, previously known for its air-hockey tables, produced the first mass-marketed Cabbage Patch Kids in 1983. Little did the executives know that by Christmas of that year they would be racing to keep up with unexpected and unprecedented demand.

As the holidays approached and the dolls became scarce, the news was filled with images of the panics that erupted in the aisles of toy stores as parents tried to get the dolls, and some people flew to Europe or even Asia just to find them.

But what made the dolls so beloved was their unique look—unlike any baby doll ever before—the pretend adoption and the promise that every doll was different, just like every child. The dolls arrived with adoption papers, and when children sent them back, the doll would get a personalized card on its first birthday.

After Coleco went out of business, Hasbro acquired the rights to produce the dolls, and later Cabbage Patch Kids became a brand of Mattel, which still produces the dolls today.

As awareness of the dolls and how they were "born" started appearing in media around the U.S., demand grew.

Babyland General Hospital came to Manhattan's Fifth Avenue, where kids could watch their unique dolls being "born" before adopting them

Hasbro's Transformers would be one of the hugest and most memorable hits of the 1980s. These transforming action figures caught kids' imaginations and established a play pattern that quickly became a classic.

Transformers were adapted from a successful line of toys from Takara in Japan, and with the Americanization of the story line, Hasbro had a megahit, with comic books (produced with Marvel Comics) and a TV series, not to mention licensed products. Kids were totally absorbed in the adventures of good guy Optimus Prime and his team of Autobots as they tried to defeat the evil Decepticons, led by Megatron.

Yet what really made these toys so exciting was the transformation. Optimus Prime was a big rig that became a powerful fighting machine, for example. With varying levels of complexity and weaponry, Transformers successfully married two favorite play patterns for boys—cars and robots.

Transformers were also featured in their own animated movie released in 1986, and in 1992, they were back in force as Hasbro introduced Generation II, which transformed into the highly successful Beast Wars. The original Transformers themselves made a comeback in 2001 as one of Hasbro's core brands—this time with more sophisticated transformations, thanks to advances in design and manufacturing over nearly twenty years.

The power of Transformers to touch the imaginations of kids would be seen again and again, particularly as adult men joyfully responded to their reintroduction in 2001. For example, a routine security check at Chicago's O'Hare airport in December 2001 turned into a virtual fan convention as an executive traveling with a Transformer in his carry-on was regaled with stories by security workers and members of the National Guard about the Transformers they had as kids...until he almost missed his plane.

Kids were totally absorbed in the adventures of good guy Optimus Prime and his team of Autobots as they tried to defeat the evil Decepticons, led by Megatron.

1984 Transformers

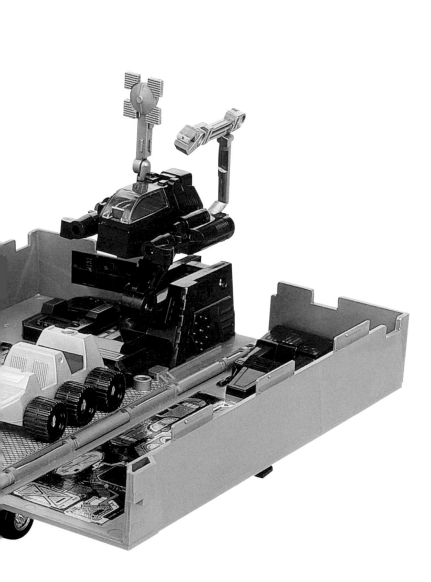

1985
Bubble Mower

Kids could be just like grown-ups, but no one had to rake up the bubbles!

Role-playing is one of the quintessential modes of play. Every kid wants to be big just like dad or mom, and there have always been role-play toys. From tools to kitchen utensils to telephones and driving toys, kids spend a lot of time practicing to be grown-ups.

Since these toys have always been part of kids' play, it's been a rare one that's really caused a sensation. But in 1985, Fisher-Price found an unlikely but perfect combination that, in its first year of production, became a million-selling role-play toy.

Now you might not think that bubbles and lawn mowers go together...but they do. The Fisher-Price Bubble Mower was an instant sensation from the moment it hit the market. For kids, it was really cool to have their own mower just like dad's that shot out a stream of bubbles and made realistic mower sounds. For adults, it was just as cute as all get-out to see the kids running around pretending to mow the lawn...or the sidewalk or the driveway.

Over the next several years, role-playing toys would become more sophisticated to reflect an ever-more-sophisticated culture and would include computers, cell phones and all the trappings of a late twentieth-century life, but the inherent appeal of the Bubble Mower (and the need to keep the lawn trimmed, no matter how busy one's life gets) has made it a best-seller since it was first introduced.

1985
My Buddy

Ever since the '60s, toy makers had been trying to create a doll for boys. That is, in addition to G.I. Joe. With the relaxing of gender stereotypes came a new awareness that maybe it was okay for preschool boys to have a playmate that could keep them company—and even be hugged. What's more, marketers had discovered that the Cabbage Patch Kids had appealed to quite a large number of boys, so perhaps the time was right to create a doll that was designed to appeal exclusively to boys.

A surprising number of people who were kids in the mid-1980s can still sing the commercial jingle that introduced My Buddy, and even if they didn't have the toy, he is remembered as a phenomenon of the period.

My Buddy had bib overalls, a striped shirt, a classic boy face and a baseball cap. The idea was that he would go everywhere with the kid and that his owner would "teach him everything I know," as the song went.

Largely because he was unique and because of the prevailing notion that it was now okay for a boy to have a doll, My Buddy enjoyed several seasons of popularity, even acquiring a Kid Sister in 1986.

Because of My Buddy's success, various companies would try to introduce dolls for boys, for wrestling and hugging and all those boy things, but none would ever generate the kind of following, friendship and fond memories My Buddy inspired for those who knew him...and love him still.

With the relaxing of gender stereotypes came a new awareness that maybe it was okay for preschool boys to have a playmate that could keep them company—and even be hugged.

Teddy Ruxpin created almost as much of a stir as did the original Teddy Bear eighty-two years earlier.

Ever since there have been dolls and stuffed animals, kids have imagined having conversations with them. These best friends were so real to so many kids that the obvious wish would be for them to come to life.

In 1985, that's exactly what happened when Worlds of Wonder introduced Teddy Ruxpin (TR), the first talking, storytelling teddy bear. Best of all, TR really seemed to talk: He had an animatronic face with a mouth and eyes that moved as the cassette tape played. (Embedded on one track of the audiotape were signals that controlled his movements.)

While Teddy Ruxpin represented a huge advance in technology within the toy industry, for kids he was just magical, and though relatively expensive at the time, TR became one of the most popular toys of the year and created almost as much of a stir as did the original Teddy Bear eighty-two years earlier. Kids didn't care that Teddy wasn't exactly huggable—they loved hav-ing their friend tell them a story.

Teddy Ruxpin and his stories became so popular that he inspired his own TV series and a line of spin-off products, though Teddy himself always remained the most popular. In 1989, Hasbro's Playskool brand acquired the license and for a brief period manufactured products under the brand.

Today, Teddy Ruxpin is still discussed in hushed tones of wonder by adults who were kids when he was first introduced. Many collect Teddy Ruxpin, and Internet chat rooms buzz with information about this beloved toy and how to keep him working. Over the years, advances in chip technology have allowed more toys to talk, to the point where it is almost commonplace. Yet nothing will ever replace the magic of that first moment when a child asked his or her teddy bear to "tell me a story"—and he did.

Is it a toy? Or a work of art? Or a toy that can be used to create works of art? These are all questions that have surrounded the abstract construction toy Zolo since its launch in 1986.

There is a certain amount of argument for the art camp, particularly as the toy was sold through the Museum of Modern Art during its first two years of distribution. It was also originally made of wood—an expensive proposition for something of such scale to be distributed through the mass market.

Subsequently, the toy was manufactured in plastic by Wild Planet Toys. What was remarkable about the translation into the new medium was that it maintained the level of whimsy and the nontraditional color and design scheme.

Zolo was, and still is, important in that it appealed to a significant portion of the toy-buying public, who haunted museum shops and specialty stores looking for those unique products that appealed to adult sensibilities of design. Zolo also appealed to consumers for its gender neutrality—in both its appearance and the kinds of play it encouraged.

Toys such as Zolo and a wide variety of educational items helped fuel the growth of specialty chains and Web sites through the '90s, and they remain important in the toy industry, as designers, entrepreneurs and small companies continue to push the design envelope to appeal to a relatively small but passionate and influential segment of the consumer market.

1987
Playmobil

Since its launch in Germany in 1974, there has always been something warm and appealing about Playmobil. The secret is all in the design. Hans Beck, who was head of design at Geobra, the company that developed the product, understood that a toy that fit a child's hands would be easier for him or her to manipulate. He knew that the scale of the toy and its environment would have to be proportional to the child, and the child should be able to relate to the toy, so in designing the original line of figures, Beck spent hours looking at children's drawings, noting the ways in which the features, particularly the head, were exaggerated.

The design went through many stages until the company got it right. Heads and arms were able to move, and every effort was made to make play physically and imaginatively accessible.

The result was a line of toys that has become tremendously popular around the world. It was launched in the specialty channels in the U.S. in 1987, and by 2000, more than 1.5 billion Playmobil pieces had been sold. Parents have consistently loved the quality, the endearing characters and the open-ended play experience, which encourages children to interact with Playmobil in whatever ways their imaginations dictate.

Now here's an unlikely group of heroes: teenage turtles who talk like surfers, fight like ninjas, play rock and roll and subsist on a diet of pizza. Doesn't sound very mainstream, does it?

In fact, the Teenage Mutant Ninja Turtles came from underground. (No, not the sewer where they lived.) Underground comic books, that is. Created by Kevin Eastman and Peter Laird in 1984, the four characters with classic names (the creators studied art history in college)—Michelangelo, Leonardo, Donatello and Raphael—were originally intended to spoof the whole action-figure, superhero genre. Instead, the Turtles became one of the biggest hits of all time.

Starting with about $1,200 and a passion for comics, the partners were able to produce 3,000 copies of their first comic book. It was a hit, and demand kept growing until they were selling more than 125,000 copies of each issue—the most successful black-and-white comic of all time.

It was at this point that people began to pay attention. In 1988, a relatively small toy company named Playmates was eager to get into the boys' action-figure category. The company liked the Turtles, but if the property was going to have mass-market appeal, there needed to be an animated TV show. A pilot was produced, and it was as successful as the comic book. Soon, the syndicated show became one of the favorites of kids around the country. They loved the comedy, the camaraderie and the Turtles, who seemed like typical teenagers—except that they were actual turtles and were trained in martial arts by a mutated rat named Splinter. The look, the attitude and the comedy were fresh and appealing, and kids couldn't get enough.

In fact, the show and the toys were so successful that they influenced the broad-based U.S. culture. Suddenly people who had never seen a killer wave were shouting "cowabunga!" and calling each other "dude." Interest in martial arts exploded, pizza sales were up, toys were flying off the shelves and kids' entertainment would never be the same.

1988
Teenage Mutant
Ninja Turtles

1989
Polly Pocket

First there was Gulliver. Then Alice in Wonderland. Then Horton the Elephant and the Whos. They've all delighted kids, and what they have in common is that they all involve miniature worlds or at least worlds that are miniature to the heroes and heroines. This fantasy allows kids to feel big in a world in which they're small.

Plus, there's something so darn cute about little things. That's part of the magic behind Mattel's Polly Pocket doll line. Mattel licensed the product, which was introduced in England by Bluebird Toys, for global distribution and set about creating a mini-doll sensation.

Polly and her friends came in a variety of fashion accessories—compacts, purses, etc. Inside, though, instead of the grown-up stuff mom carried was a magical world filled with color and excitement, all in miniature. Girls began collecting them by the scores, and even the Barbie doll had her own Polly Pocket collection for a while.

Soon, Polly Pocket didn't just have a world, she had a universe. Mattel created Fashion Polly (who was slightly larger) and many accessories. Clearly, the magic of the miniatures has woven its spell. By 2002, Polly and the entire mini-doll category were continuing to delight little girls in a big, big way.

Polly let kids feel big in a world in which they're small.

1991
K'NEX Ferris
Wheel

Original model for K'NEX

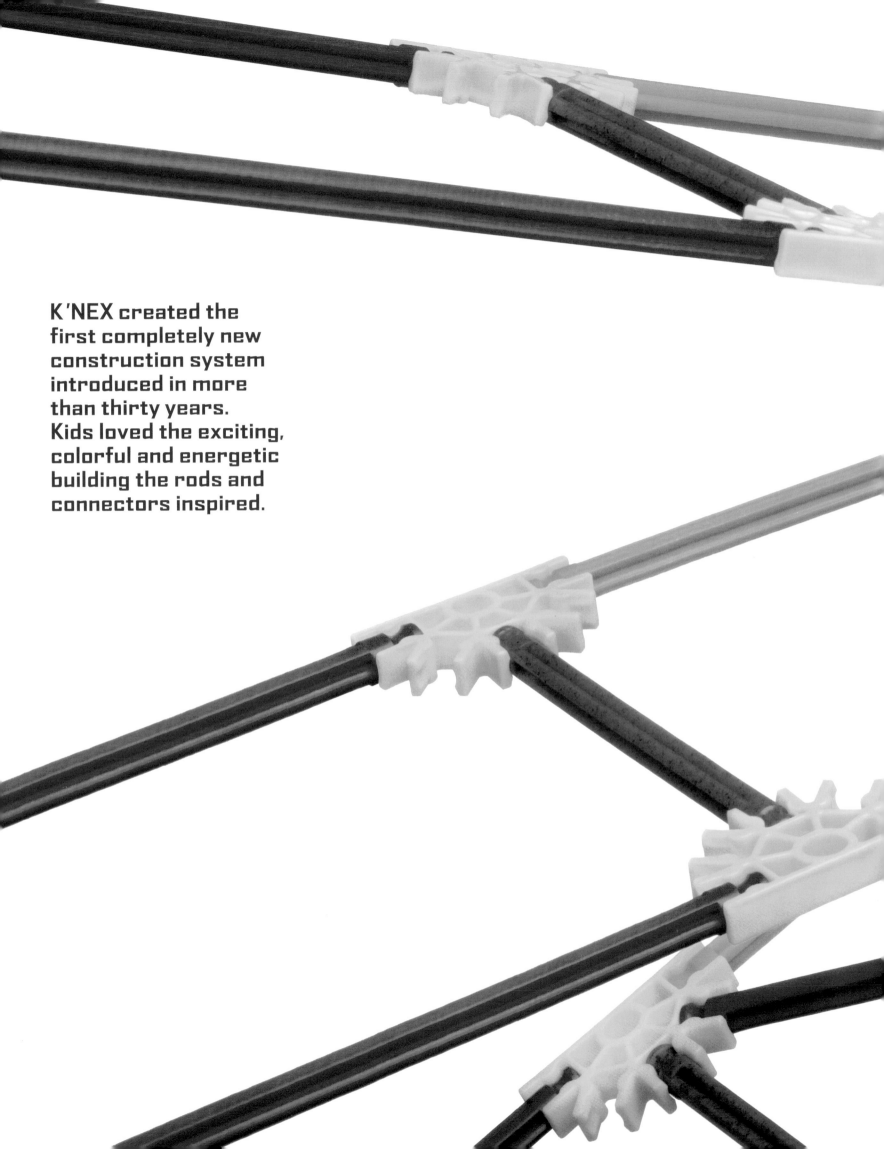

K'NEX created the
first completely new
construction system
introduced in more
than thirty years.
Kids loved the exciting,
colorful and energetic
building the rods and
connectors inspired.

Joel Glickman was not the first person to be bored at a wedding. Nor was he the first person to distract himself from the proceedings, thereby avoiding doing the Chicken Dance, by stringing together cocktail straws. What was different about Glickman was that he was the CEO of the Rodon Group, a plastics injection-molding company that had created many innovative products in the automotive and pharmaceutical industries...not to mention inventing those little plastic "tables" that keep the box top from collapsing on your delivery pizza.

As Glickman sat idly bending straws, he had the idea that what was so engaging to him might make an engaging construction toy. Over the next year, he designed and experimented, ultimately creating an entire system of colorful rods and connectors that would allow kids to create three-dimensional models.

Coming up with a solid product idea is one thing, but bringing it to market is another. In the toy industry, the construction sector had been particularly slow, with one or two classic toys capturing most of the sales. TV advertising was prohibitively expensive for introducing a new toy. So how to communicate the excitement and, most important, the possibilities of building with what was now called K'NEX?

Glickman created an electrically driven eight-foot Ferris wheel that was displayed at stores. (Kids could build a ten-inch version with their building sets, driven by a hand crank and a rubber band.) The huge models captured imaginations and over the next few years K'NEX did what many thought was impossible—establish a new building system within the construction category.

2002

The final decade of the century was in many ways a fitting summary of everything that had gone before. On the one hand, hearth and home were more important than ever. On the other hand, technology had completely transformed virtually everything about the ways in which we communicated, did business and played. Cable channels and satellite television boomed, movie theaters multiplied into multiplexes and niche marketing sought to create something for everyone—something uniquely tailored to a specific group of individuals, that is. ■ But nothing would affect the culture as much as the Internet. By the end of the decade, nearly

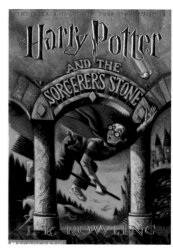
Harry Potter, 1999

100 million people worldwide were connected to the Internet. It may not have transformed business—as the dot-com crash of 2000 showed—but it had linked the world and facilitated communication as nothing before it had. ■ Politically it was, once again, a time of upheaval. The Gulf War began the decade, and the U.S. was involved more broadly around the world militarily than it had

1993-2002 The Information Age Comes Home

been in many years. At home there were political scandals, the bombing of the Federal building in Oklahoma City and the 1993 terrorist attack on the World Trade Center. And worst of all, on September 11, 2001, terrorists attacked the World Trade Center and the Pentagon, provoking a national reaction of shock and grief, along with a renewed sense of patriotism and national purpose. ■ Through most of the decade, the economy boomed, which gave Americans more disposable income than at any previous

Scooter, 2000

time. More people invested in the stock market than ever before and optimism ran high until it collapsed in 2000, when the economy went into a recession. ■ Kids growing up in a technological world abandoned traditional toys at earlier ages than ever before. While adults disputed the issue, kids eagerly embraced new technologies and new experiences, and were for the most part better equipped than at any time in history to face the challenges of the information age. ■ Fashion ran the gamut from hip-hop styles for young people to a generally more casual look for everyone else. Businesses instituted dress-down Fridays, and in all but the most formal industries, the gray flannel suit was a relic of the past.

A tourist in Times Square views a Nasdaq ticker, 2001

■ Music was dominant within youth culture, especially with young kids. Groups such as *NSYNC, Destiny's Child, the Backstreet Boys and Boyz II Men and singers such as Britney Spears, Christina Aguilera, Jennifer Lopez and many others defined a new pop sound that appealed to young girls. These girls flooded concert halls, dressed like their idols and sang karaoke to their favorite songs. ■ The home rental market for films boomed, and home videos played a role in supporting toy lines and allowing parents greater control over their children's entertainment. ■ Television reached ninety-nine percent of U.S. homes, the majority of which had two or more televisions. Reality shows kept the nation riveted and made it possible for average people to

Cast of "Friends" at the Emmy awards, 2002

become stars—no matter how far they had to go to do it. CNN changed the way we got news—it was instant and ongoing, and entertainment pushed the envelope further, introducing previously unthinkable subject matter. ■ Technology affected every aspect of the toy industry—and virtually every product. By 2002, nearly eighty percent of all preschool products had some kind of chip in them. Parents who were focused on—not to say obsessed by—their children's education leapt at anything that would seem to enhance their tots' abilities. Companies like VTech helped children learn the basics with precomputers, and handheld games and robotics

Teenage fashion, mobile phone, 2001

reflected the technological world children lived in. ■ Throughout the decade, licenses and entertainment properties continued to perform very well—Harry Potter, Pokémon, SpongeBob SquarePants, Rugrats, Blue's Clues, Sesame Street. ■ But technology didn't shut out the classics: The toy box just expanded to accommodate new types of products. There was a growing interest in arts and crafts, and the specialty market was alive with small companies emphasizing quality design. It was all about the quality of the play experience, and kids didn't care whether something was technologically

iMac computer, 2002

enhanced or not, as long as it was fun. Thus, all the high-tech toys—games like Magic: The Gathering, which ran on the classic elements of cards and imagination—existed side by side with electronic marvels. As with so much else, there was something for everyone. ■ Dolls got more fashion-forward, reflecting the culture's greater sophistication, which naturally filtered down to young girls. Toy cars had astonishing performance; chips created reality as it could not have been imagined by the great-great-grandparents of children at the beginning of the twentieth century.

■ Yet one thing remained the same: Play was still the most powerful way for children to explore, discover and engage their worlds.

1993
Mighty Morphin
Power Rangers

It was the ultimate kid fantasy. You were granted special powers to dispel evil in the guise of really creepy buggy robotic monster thingies.

They have been one of the best-selling action figure lines of all time, with toy sales counted in the billions. The Mighty Morphin Power Rangers introduced a new generation of kids to the power and appeal of the martial arts.

The TV show had a unique live-action format with plenty of special effects, as ordinary teens "morphed" into the Red, Blue, Yellow, White and Black Rangers. It was the ultimate kid fantasy. You were granted special powers to dispel evil in the guise of really creepy buggy robotic monster thingies. Every battle was an ultimate battle, for the Power Rangers seemed to live and fight at a constant fever pitch.

Kids caught that fever and couldn't wait to play Power Rangers, and suddenly martial-arts play swept the country. Bandai's toys were an instant hit, and the really cool thing about them was that not only did the toys morph, but you could put them all together to create ultimate Mega-Zords. And even saying their names is fun. Try this: "Deluxe Quantasaurus Mega-Zord, the Ultimate Zord of the Quantum Ranger!" Don't you feel more powerful already?

Like the Teenage Mutant Ninja Turtles before them, the Power Rangers captured the imagination of kids and held it for years. Each year since their third season, the Power Rangers have gone on new adventures with new themes. Kids who are deeply into the Power Rangers of today are discovering the older, "classic" Power Rangers, and very often digging their big brothers' toys out of the basement.

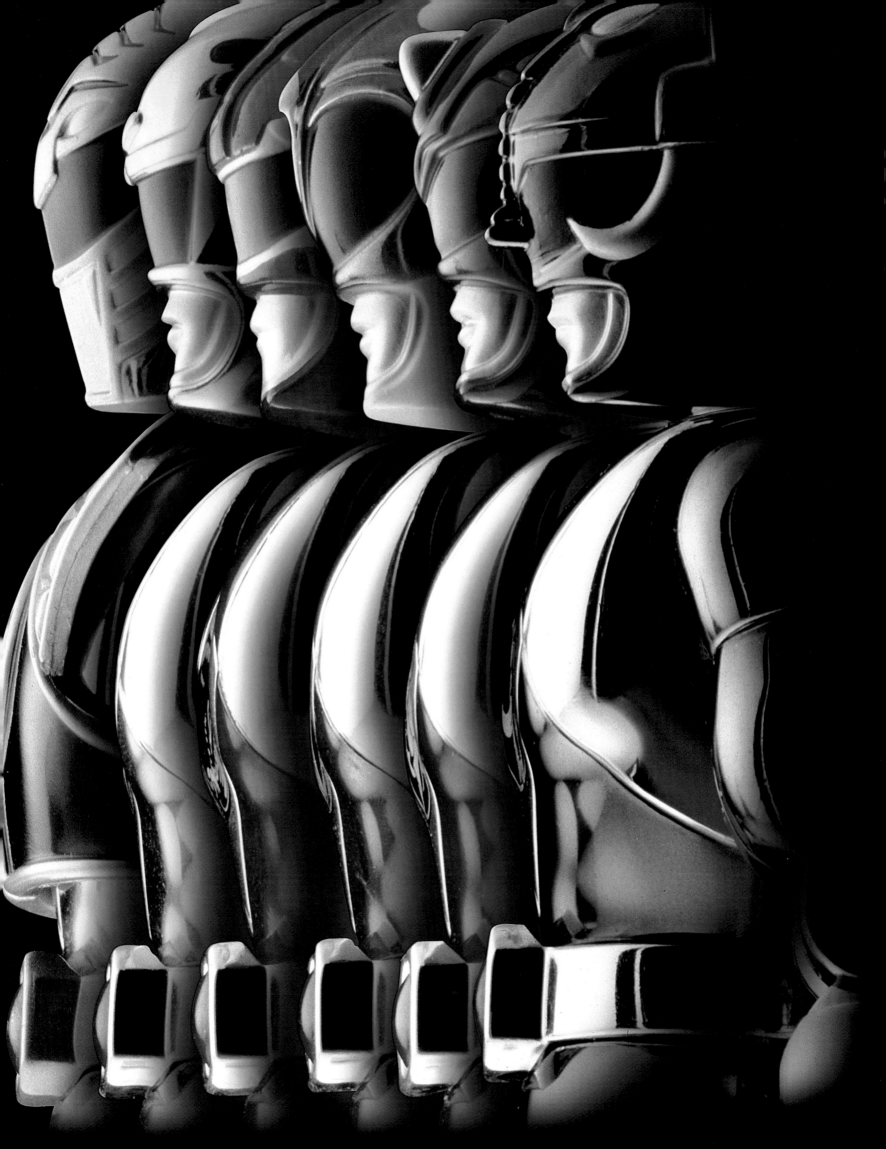

1995 Rebound

Rebound had everything! Speed, maneuverability and a way out of situations that would stop a lesser R/C vehicle.

In the early 1990s, radio control was largely for the hobbyist. Drivers were concerned with speed first and foremost, and then replicas. But companies like Tyco realized that there was a significant market for more toylike radio-controlled cars (R/C) that would appeal to kids...and adults who liked to play like kids. Tyco was also one of the first companies to make the cars more affordable, and the company developed advanced battery technology so cars could charge faster and run longer, which made them more appealing to their owners.

Tyco had introduced a variety of cars that met all these criteria and did some cool stunts. The trouble was they could get stuck or stranded. In 1995, the company launched Rebound, and it changed R/C design forever.

For the first time, there was an R/C car that had four-wheel drive. If it hit a wall or an obstacle, a few deft manipulations of the remote control got it free. The car could flip, spin and bounce off anything it encountered, and it was good in virtually any terrain. With the introduction of Rebound, the R/C category became more focused on features and stunts, something that would continue into the twenty-first century. There would be more vehicles and more technology (including gyroscopes that helped R/C motorcycles stay up without cumbersome supports), which fueled a growing category.

Because it was so cool and new, and did so much, Rebound became the top-selling vehicle in both 1995 and 1996, and it raised the bar on R/C design.

TRY ME!
Squeeze My
Right Hand Or
Hug My
Tummy!

SAYS
HUNDREDS
OF
PHRASES!

Barney

Barney
PLAYSKOOL

EVEREADY. Super Heavy
Duty brand batteries included

71245

1995 Talking Barney

He's big. He's purple. He's always happy. He has a voice that can set some adults' teeth on edge. But no matter what grown-ups say, millions of children around the world consider Barney their very best friend.

Barney the dinosaur hit the market in 1987 as a series of videotapes created by Sheryl Leach, a former teacher who was committed to creating strong educational experiences for preschoolers. So Barney danced and sang and said really happy things like "Super-dee-dooper!" and charmed virtually every kid he encountered. (And if he didn't appeal to adults, even the grumpiest had to admit that teaching children to say "please" and "thank you" and to be good friends isn't a bad thing.)

The always upbeat prehistoric playmate was innocent and silly, and kids could instantly relate to him. He could be goofy and gentle—and, of course, he was oh-so-huggable. Barney became a business powerhouse, spawning a magazine, a sold-out traveling show and, in 1995, a line of toys from Hasbro.

Talking Barney was the star of the first line—as cuddly as the real thing and able to say hundreds of different phrases. This was one of the first applications of talking-chip technology, which allowed toys to say more and more to their human friends. Talking Barney ushered in a new era in talking toys—a long way from the pull-string—that would shape preschool products from that point forward.

Despite his adult detractors, who made Barney the butt of jokes and satire—and incidentally helped build his fame—Barney remains one of the most popular preschool characters of the century. Even a study commissioned by Yale University found that each Barney TV show had more than 150 "teaching moments" and was an effective, entertaining preschool learning tool.

But kids don't think about that. They just know that they love Barney—and they'll keep loving him...no matter what any grown-up says.

1995
Gooey Louie

There comes a time in nearly every child's life when bodily functions—the grosser the better—represent the absolute pinnacle of humor. While adults may feel a little bit squeamish, this kind of play is all very natural as children discover their bodies and learn appropriate behaviors. Most of all, though, gross humor has a rich history in comedy throughout the ages.

Every few years since the 1960s there have been toys that capitalize on this phase and usher in a new era of "gross" toys. In the mid-1990s, the cycle came around again, and Pressman Toy introduced a game that was aptly and accurately—named Gooey Louie.

Louie was in the vein of the so-called "skill-and-action" games and was perfectly targeted to an eight-year-old's sense of humor and the ridiculous. It took the "naughty" habit of picking one's nose and made it into a game. Simply put, the goal was to pull the most "gooies" out of Louie's nose without getting the one that would make his head pop open and his brain fly out. Once that happened, you reset the game and did it all over again. It was like a cartoon that came to life—at least that's how kids saw it.

Perhaps you had to be there to get the full impact of the comedy, but kids adored this game, partially because of Louie's silly, cartoonish appearance. As with the best of the gross toys, Louie had an inherent innocence that allowed children to laugh at the action and at themselves. That laughter helped make Gooey Louie the best-selling game in its category for the year.

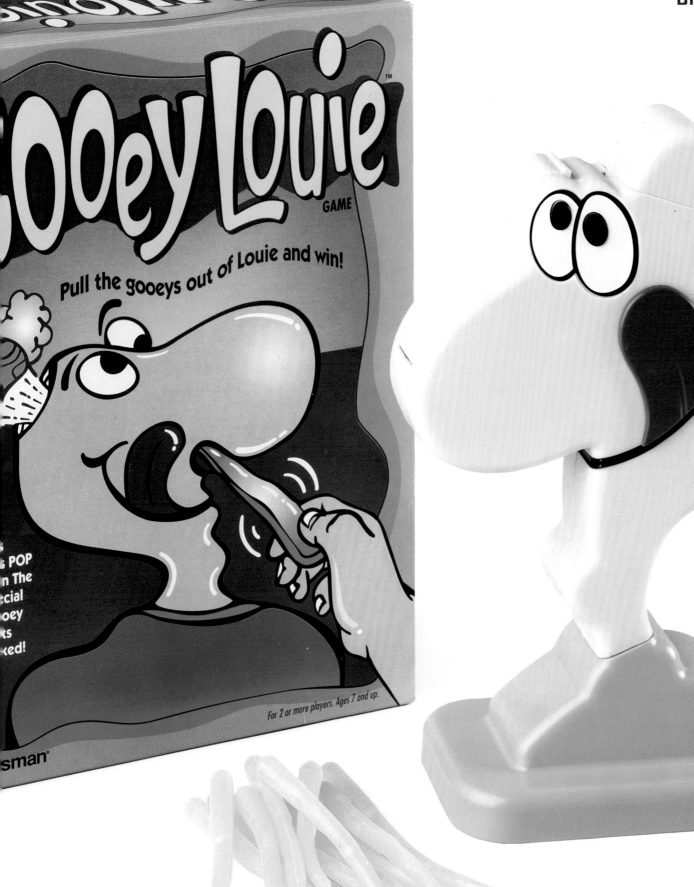

"Pick his nose till his
brain explodes."

1996
Bass Fishin'

Radica used motion sensors to create a new kind of game—and opened the door to a whole new category of handheld electronic games.

Perhaps in reaction to fast-paced lifestyles, in the late '90s, fishing emerged as an entertainment phenomenon with the expansion of cable broadcasting and the success of shows such as "Bass Masters." Sure it was a niche market, but it was enormous.

Fisherman and game designer Bob Davids knew that there were people out there who couldn't get enough fishing, and he set out to design a game that would allow players to simulate the fishing experience, even if they were nowhere near a stream.

Of course, Davids had a little bit of an advantage when it came to creating such a game. As one of the founders of Radica, he had built a successful electronic games business, but what he was about to do had never been done before.

Instead of the static handheld electronic game, Davids and his team created a unit that looked like the handle of a fishing rod, complete with reel and crank, with an LCD screen at the top of the handle. Players first chose the lake, then selected bait (which was dependent on weather conditions) and then cast. You could see the fish swimming below, and the goal was to catch as many as possible—the prize being the twenty-five pound "lunker." When you hooked a fish, you actually felt the game shake, and you had to reel it in carefully, so as not to break or snag the line. Players were amazed at the level of realism, the game was a huge hit and, during the first year, with a few programming tweaks, it became even more real with random probabilities built in—just like in real sport fishing.

In addition to selling more than fifteen million games, Davids and Radica had created a new category within the handheld game industry. Over the next several years, Radica and other companies raced into production a whole variety of virtual-reality handhelds, which all had motion sensors and tactile feedback built into the game.

As popular as all of these other games were, Bass Fishin' remained the dominant player in the category and has been continually updated with new challenges and more action. It's a market phenomenon that didn't get away, and that's no fish story.

He made his first national TV appearance with Al Roker on the "Today Show" in February 1996, but before the holidays of that year, he would be headline news and a seasoned TV celebrity in the U.S. and around the world. Oh sure, there had been toy crazes before (Shirley Temple Dolls, Hula Hoops, Cabbage Patch), but no single toy had ever so delighted the nation or caused such a consumer frenzy. In addition to entertaining two-year-olds (his primary purpose), Tickle Me Elmo changed the way Americans looked at toys during the holidays, causing nearly every media outlet in the country to race to be first to anoint the "hot toy" of the year every year.

Tickle Me Elmo started out quietly—not as Elmo at all, but as a monkey who laughed and giggled. When Tyco Preschool acquired the rights to produce toys based on the "Sesame Street" characters, Elmo, with his infectious manner and runaway popularity, was the natural choice for the first use of the technology. Tickle Me Elmo was also significant in that it was the first pre-school toy that was advertised exclusively to adults in prime time.

Embraced by Rosie O'Donnell, Bryant Gumbel and *USA Today,* and front-page news on virtually every paper around the nation, this giggling doll became the must-have of the season. People were spending thousands of dollars for it. Even Cartier had Elmo in its window, and the fabulous diamond necklace draped around his neck was free...to the person who bought the doll for a million bucks. (Someone did.) There were stories of toy desperados stealing Elmos from the checked luggage of travelers, staking out the loading docks of toy stores and bribing clerks in attempts to snag this prize.

Of course, as with all fads, the furor passed and Tickle Me Elmo settled into life as an enduring preschool classic.

1996
Tickle Me Elmo

Cartier had Elmo in its window, and the fabulous diamond necklace draped around his neck was free...to the person who bought the doll for a million bucks.

In the late '90s, the specialty toy market boomed, and with it a new awareness of the power of specialty stores within the industry and the need for unique product available only through these channels. At the same time, the growth of specialty chain stores, including Noodle Kidoodle and Zany Brainy, created nationwide outlets for high quality, often uniquely creative product lines targeted to specific groups of toy buyers. As a result, the strategy of niche marketing was increasingly adopted within the toy industry. At the same time, more and more parents and caregivers sought these products, and smaller companies like Manhattan Toy grew on the strength of these niche markets.

In 1997, the company created a breakthrough line of dolls with a look and feel that girls readily responded to: Groovy Girls were soft fabric dolls with a very fashionable look and equally cool furniture. Girls started collecting these handmade, artist dolls with funky style like crazy. At once old-fashioned and fashion-forward, the dolls reflected much of the decade's aesthetic, as well as a message about diversity.

In the ensuing years, the mass market would bring a hipper sense of fashion to dolls, with nearly twenty lines of so-called "attitude" dolls shown at the Toy Fair in 2002, and this new look all started with the Groovy Girls.

250

Girls started collecting these handmade, artist dolls with funky style like crazy.

1997 Groovy Girls

1998
Spy Vision
Goggles

Throughout the century, kids have played at being heroes. It's exciting. Particularly since the cold war, spy play has been extremely popular. Not only were spies in the news, they figured in entertainment as well, starting with *The Man from U.N.C.L.E.* and James Bond and continuing through many other high-profile superspies, who always, thanks to intelligence and cool gadgets, managed to defeat the enemy.

From the earliest decoder rings and disappearing ink to some very sophisticated toys at the end of the century, kids have always loved toy spy gear that allowed them to pretend they had superior powers. By 1998, this had become an established play pattern.

That was the year that Wild Planet gave kids an exciting new power: the ability to see in the dark. The Spy Vision Goggles combined futuristic styling with working high-tech night vision. Wild Planet successfully adapted aviator goggles and added green night-vision lenses, which allowed kids to see up to twenty-five feet in the dark. Suddenly there was a new level of realism in make-believe missions, and a new level of drama was added to a classic mode of play.

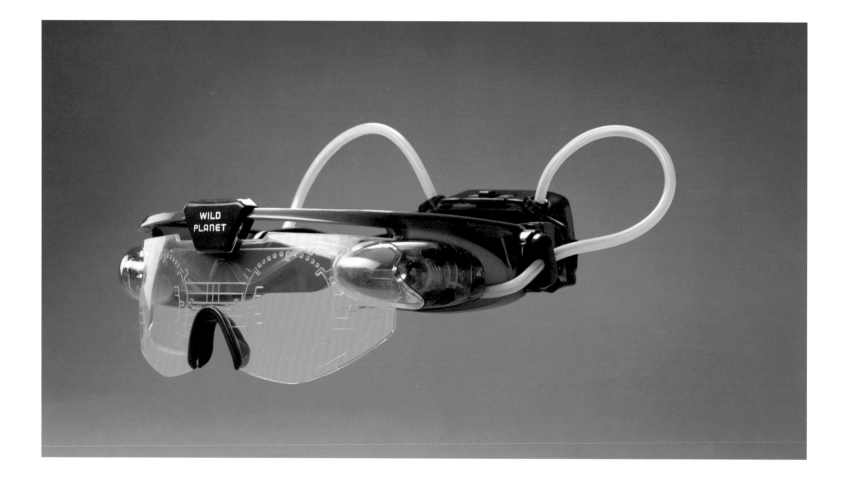

Kids loved seeing in the dark—perfect for after-hours missions.

As so often happens, a small, relatively new company would prove conventional wisdom wrong and open up a new category in the toy industry.

The Air Hogs Sky Shark was the first of its kind. Developed by British inventors John Dickson and Peter Manning, the Sky Shark used a one-piston, air-compression engine to power its propeller and allow it to fly more than a hundred yards. Kids simply pumped it up and let it go. The Sky Shark didn't just fly, it flew really well, and kids everywhere wanted to experience the magic and power of this unique model plane. More than five million planes were sold, making the Sky Shark one of the best-selling toys of the year.

And wouldn't you know...suddenly there was a flying-toy category, and other companies jumped into the business. Now hooked on flight, Spin Master and other toy companies would keep pushing the envelope, adding elements such as radio control and more complex engines. Over the next several years, sophisticated flying toys would populate the market, and consumers would make them fly off toy shelves.

Before Air Hogs, flying toys had been limited to the hobby category, and enthusiasts spent hundreds of dollars or more on sophisticated models. Advances in technology and reduced production costs put the power and fascination with flight within the reach of virtually everyone.

1998 Air Hogs

A young pilot gets ready to launch his
Air Hogs plane from the Wright Brothers
memorial in Kitty Hawk

1998 Betty Spaghetty

Original model for Betty Spaghetty

Before 1998, many manufacturers had looked for ways to enter the fashion-doll category. They had tried very hard to get a piece of this lucrative market, but none had created any long-term success. Toy inventor Elonne Dantzer took a long look at the category and realized that what was needed was not another traditional fashion doll, but something completely different that could complement what was already being offered and allow girls to build on their love of fashion and role-play with a totally new doll-play pattern.

And so, as many toy inventors did, she started making the rounds with a prototype. It was a fairly prosaic construction of pipe cleaners and a Ping-Pong ball, to be sure, and it would probably have taken a lot of imagination to envision what was being called Betty Spaghetty as a viable toy.

Many, in fact, could not. Yet as so often happens, it was a company that had never been in the doll business and never tried to be in the doll business that was able to see what Betty could become. Ohio Art decided to take a chance, and under the creative guidance of Josephine Wood—very much in the tradition of classic movies—the girl that no one had really noticed became a star.

Launched at the Toy Fair in 1988, Betty Spaghetty became one of the toys everyone was talking about. Her hip and funky look perfectly captured the way young girls were dressing or wanted to dress. Now every girl wants to be well put together, and that's literally how they played with Betty, assembling dolls from a variety of arms, legs, outfits and the all-important fashion accessories. Each creation was a unique expression of little girls' imaginations, and they fell in love with her.

Betty sold very well in the United States, is a major hit internationally and is becoming a classic. Significantly, she also opened the door for the hip, trendy looks that would characterize new entries in the doll category at the beginning of the twenty-first century. And all it took was a little imagination and great design, as with any star.

1998 Furby

Those eyes!
That voice!
He was a star—
the must-have
toy of the year.

He wasn't exactly cute, but he wasn't ugly either.
What he was, however, was a phenomenon.
In the late '90s, technology toys experienced
a boom, and with the success of virtual pets
(Tamagotchi, Giga Pets and all sort of others),
a new market was born.

Tiger Electronics, which had emerged as one
of the leading electronic toy companies, saw the
opportunity to take what had essentially been
an LCD game on a key chain and turn it into a
dimensional best friend. The result was Furby,
a furry creature with adorable eyes, who actually
learned more and got smarter the more kids
played with him. He started out speaking his own
language, "Furbish," but over time would speak
in English. The more you did with him, the more
he did, and people couldn't get enough of him.

In fact, Furby was the year's must-have fad
toy. Not since Tickle Me Elmo had there been a
toy that was so sought-after and so newsworthy.
Consumers who remembered missing out on
Elmo started lining up outside stores at four in
the morning to be sure of scoring a Furby. For
the second time in as many years, a toy and consumers' quest for that toy was the lead story on
virtually every evening news broadcast.

Of course, some people thought Furby could
actually hear them, and among other possibly
apocryphal stories that circulated was the one
about government offices that didn't want Furby
on the premises because he might learn confi-
dential secrets and cause leaks. (Though "ah-way,
ooh-way, da-hay," which he literally said, might
have been hard to decode.)

The success of Furby created the entire interactive pet category. Over the next several years,
Tiger followed up Furby with Furby Babies, ultimately selling more than forty million of these
computerized critters.

These everyday heroes became the first preschool action figures—and a huge hit.

1998 Rescue Heroes

Action figures are virtually as old as play. Accounts of ancient Greece include children playing with miniature soldiers they had fashioned themselves. The modern action-figure category, however, really dates to 1963 and the introduction of the G.I. Joe line, in which characters helped guide and inspire children's natural storytelling and dramatic play.

For nearly thirty-five years, though, most action figures had been themed around the classic boy play pattern of power and conflict, and had themes related to war, space and lots of abstract battles between good guys and bad guys. While parents certainly bought these figures, seemingly by the ton, mothers especially wished that action figures, and especially the good guys, more reflected the real world in which their kids were growing up.

Fisher-Price responded in 1988 with the launch of Rescue Heroes. Based on firefighters, police and other rescue workers, these figures answered the call. In addition to its wholesome, real-world themes, Rescue Heroes was the first action-figure line designed specifically for preschoolers.

As often happens in the preschool category, the growth of the line was steady. Over time the line grew to comprise more than forty different characters and became the second best-selling line of action figures in 2001. More than nine million Rescue Heroes were sold between 1998 and 2001. Not bad for a group of hometown heroes who have absolutely no alien menaces to conquer!

It was in the wake of the September 11 tragedy in 2001, though, that Rescue Heroes took center stage in the U.S. With a new focus on rescue—and a new respect for real-life heroes—Fisher-Price's special New York Fire Department (FDNY) version of their popular character Billy Blazes raised more than $1 million with Toys "R" Us and became a symbol of hope and heroism.

As the twentieth century drew to a close, reading and reading readiness became hot-button issues, particularly for parents in the U.S. There was growing concern that children might not be effectively equipped to handle the competitive academic and professional worlds they would one day enter.

Computer chips met creativity, and manufacturers responded with a whole new category of toys that came to be called ELAs (Electronic Learning Aids). Suddenly kids could reinforce skills at the punch of a button, and many companies jumped into the category.

Yet in 1995, lawyer Mike Wood was dissatisfied with many of the options available to help him teach his young son phonics. Working with Dr. Robert Calfee, professor emeritus of education at Stanford University, along with other early childhood learning experts, he began developing successful phonics products, and LeapFrog Enterprises was born.

In 1999, Wood and his team created what would become the best-selling toy in the U.S. for two years running—the LeapPad Learning System. Using a combination of whole-word and phonics reading, children interacted with different books: An electronic pen was connected to the LeapPad and when children touched it to the pages of the books, they got help with their reading, played games, tested their knowledge and became deeply involved in the material in ways that would have been unimaginable just a few years earlier.

A new form of reading had arrived...just in time for the new century.

Revolutionary
technology helped
kids learn—and learn
to love—reading.

1999 LeapPad

pot

Leap gave a pat,
a tap, a rap.
Her tooth did tip.
He saw the gap.

LeapPad™
LEARNING SYSTEM

In the last years of the twentieth century, some researchers postulated that listening to music—and Mozart in particular—could help children improve memory. It was an idea that prompted all kinds of excitement—not to mention inspiring whole lines of products targeted to infants and preschoolers, creating a new focus on, and market for, educational toys.

Thus, it was in 1997 that Brooke Abercrombie and John Sosoka traded in their backgrounds as educational software pioneers to develop new technology-based toys that would use the latest research on learning styles to create products. The result was Neurosmith—a company that has consistently won awards for excellence, quality and strikingly beautiful design. The Music Blocks was one of the company's first breakthrough products. By arranging the blocks, children created music and learned through exploration, building the foundation for the development of higher-level cognitive skills.

Oh, and did we mention how much fun these toys are? With virtually endless opportunities for invention, even Mozart would have been impressed.

Mozart would have been impressed by the versatility and creative possibilities of Neurosmith's groundbreaking toy.

Painting of musician Wolfgang Amadeus Mozart (1756–1791) aged seven, by Pietro Antonio Lorenzoni, in the Mozarteum, Salzburg, Austria.

The toy industry went to the dogs as Poo-Chi inspired a new fascination with robots—and robotic pets.

With the new century about to dawn, robots were on everyone's mind again. No, they hadn't replaced humans as science-fiction writers had predicted fifty years earlier, but they were still fascinating and fun as all get-out.

Fresh from its success with Furby, Tiger Electronics introduced Poo-Chi—an interactive robotic dog that could do all kinds of cool things when his owner taught (programmed) him. Poo-Chi, with his big bright eyes and many moods and play modes, fascinated kids of all ages. Here was a playmate that was about as realistic as a robotic dog could be. He could sing to you. He had a full range of emotions—from delighted to cranky. He could play games. He could even do tricks! For many kids, Poo-Chi became a kind of starter pet, the next best thing to a real dog. For millions more, he captured a distinct end-of-century style that married technology and personality, the science of robotics and the emotional power of a real pet. Like so many toys that had gone before and will come after, Poo-Chi represented the best of fun in the context of the culture at the time.

2000 Poo-Chi

These creatures from an imaginary world fired up kids' imaginations in 2000.

At the beginning of the twenty-first century, one of the big buzzwords was "convergence." In other words, things that existed in one medium could exist in another as well, and they'd all work together to create something else that was even bigger.

While toy companies had tried to combine toys, the Internet, publishing and licensing in one integrated brand, the results had been inconsistent. Sitting at the computer wasn't always harmonious with much more active figure-play. But then, in 2001, came Bionicle. This story-based property seamlessly integrated various forms of media, for the first time maintaining the utilitarian integrity of each. Thus, kids went to a Web site or a comic book to discover more about the story. They played with the figures alone and with friends in traditional action-figure play and then encountered other products, which were always related to the story.

Now, to an adult, the story is quite complex and rather confusing, but it made complete sense to kids, who immersed themselves in the world of the Bionicle characters. And while these characters, called Toah, required some assembly, this was a huge departure from LEGO, which was known for its more linear construction systems.

Bionicle once again reinforced the essential importance of story to children's fantasy play—that it is the springboard to new worlds of excitement and fun for kids. It reinforces the concept that play is unique for each child and that a plastic toy, a Web site or any other element is only a catalyst for the imagination. It is, and always has been, the imagination that has the power.

Child development, virtually from birth, was becoming an increasingly important issue to parents at the beginning of the twenty-first century. A whole category of the toy industry now focused on creating infant and preschool items that would combine entertainment with research-based elements to help foster and support a baby's development. Concurrently, toy designers were using new materials and bolder colors and fabrics. These toys did especially well at specialty stores that catered to parents and caregivers looking for toys to help stimulate development.

Learning Curve combined the well-known Lamaze name with a whole line of innovative toys designed to stimulate babies' growing senses. In particular, the Littles Playtime Pals combined a variety of puppet characters and different play activities (peek-a-boo, textures and more) that would foster children's exploration and learning.

The Lamaze brand of toys was among the first that attempted both to create engaging toys for the first year of life and to help parents understand and participate in their children's growth and discovery of the world around them.

The Lamaze line of
toys represented a
new focus on child
development.

2001
FDNY Engine Co. 68

This truck is more than a toy—it's a symbol of our best selves and our strongest, most positive beliefs.

After the tragedies of September 11, 2001, the world was changed. Yet the U.S. was resilient and, though irrevocably altered, life went on. After the first days and weeks of shock, people slowly began to refocus on other aspects of their lives, and that meant play, as well.

For children play was healing, allowing them to begin to come to terms with and build a context for their altered reality. For adults, it meant paying tribute to the heroes of 9/11 and celebrating those essential characteristics of American culture that can withstand even the toughest trials.

Perhaps no group has been more honored and respected in the aftermath of 9/11 than the Fire Department of New York City (FDNY). Code 3 Collectibles has had a relationship with the FDNY since 1998, and after 9/11 their realistic replica trucks were more desirable than ever before.

For 2002, the company created the Yankees Bronx Bombers No. 68, an exact 1:32-scale replica of the truck based at Engine Company 68 in Bronx, New York. It is responsible for protecting Yankee Stadium and the surrounding areas and proudly displays the logos of the New York Yankees baseball team.

But this fire truck is more than merely a model or a toy. It is more than a symbol of local and national pride. It stands, as all toys ultimately do, as a tribute to the creative spirit, and to the power of imagination that endows those toys with relevance and meaning, life and laughter. It is a reflection of the lifelong and undeniably human quest to be the best we can be.

It is the very essence of the power of play.

Toy Industry Association, Inc.

Mission Statement

The mission of Toy Industry Association, Inc., is to promote industry growth globally and to ensure the industry's right to market and manufacture fun, educational and safe products to all ages in a free and fair manner, and in so doing support the positive development of children. To accomplish this mission TIA will:

Create member-driven programs to achieve industry growth and improve profitability

Position the industry as an advocacy group for children

Educate parents, caregivers and others about the importance of play and the safe use of toys

Broaden the membership base and establish strategic alliances and affiliations with others closely connected to the toy industry to promote growth and profitability for all

Implement communications systems to support members in all facets of their businesses

Facilitate ongoing programs for members to create awareness of and access to new technology

Represent the industry before all governments and nongovernment organizations

Support the production of safe toys in factories operated under lawful and ethical standards and in compliance with the Code of Business Practices of the International Council of Toy Industries

Lead the industry's commitment to protecting the environment

Adopted May 16, 2000

TIA Member Companies

4Kidz, Inc.

A Wish Come True

Accoutrements

Action Products International, Inc.

ADPAC Corporation

Adventure Publishing Group/Toy Book

ALEX (Panline USA, Inc.)

Alexander Doll Company, Inc.

Alfa's Fuzzy Town, Inc.

Alpi International Ltd.

Amela Corporation

American Plastic Toys, Inc.

Anjar Company

Aristoplay, Ltd.

Arlington Hat Company, Inc.

Artbox Entertainment

Aurora World, Inc. (A & A Plush, Inc.)

Avon Products, Inc.

B. Dazzle, Inc.

B. Little & Company

B.J. Toys

Bachmann Industries, Inc.

Bakery Crafts (Jack Guttman, Inc.)

Bandai America, Inc.

The Barber Group

Basic Fun, Inc.

Battat, Inc./Adica Pongo, Inc.

The Beadery Craft Products
(Div. of Greene Plastics Corp.)

Bernard Loomis, Inc.

Bestever, Inc.

Big Time Toys, L.L.C.

Binary Arts Corporation

Binney & Smith, Inc.

Blue Box Toys, Inc.

Bradford Novelty Co., Inc.

Breslow Morrison Terzian & Assoc., Inc.

Briarpatch, Inc.

BRIO Corporation

Bruder Toys America, Inc.

Bullyland, Inc.

Cadaco, Inc.
(Division of Rapid Mounting & Finishing)

Cardinal Industries, Inc.

Carolyn Forsman Bead Weaver, Ltd.

Carrom Company

Castle Toy, Inc.

Center Enterprises, Inc.

Challenge & Fun, Inc.

Chicco U.S.A., Inc.

Children's Entertainment Association

Children's Leisure Products, L.L.C.

Colart Americas, Inc.

Commodore Manufacturing Corp.

Commonwealth Toy & Novelty Co., Inc.

Comus USA, Inc.

Consumer Testing Laboratories, Inc.

Craft House International

Creative Consumer Concepts

Creative Designs Int'l, Ltd.

Creative Education of Canada, Inc.

Crocodile Creek

Curiosity Kits, Inc.

Dan-Dee International, Ltd.

Dimensions/Perler

Disguise, Inc.

The Doll Factory, Inc.

Dowling Magnet Company

Dr. Toy's Guide

DSI Toys, Inc.

Duncan Toys Company
(Division of Flambeau Products Corp.)

Eddy & Martin Goldfarb & Assoc., L.L.C.

Educational Insights, Inc.

Edushape Ltd.

Elliot Handler

Emerging Playthings

Enchanted Moments

Endless Games

Fantazzmo Fun Stuff

Fiesta

First Act, Inc.

The First Years, Inc.

Fisher-Price Brands

Fleer Collectibles

Franklin Sports, Inc.

Fun 4 All

Fun World
(Div. of Easter Unlimited, Inc.)

Funopolis, Inc.

Funrise, Inc.

Funtastic

Galt America

Game Development Group, Inc.

Games for All Reasons

GameSource Ltd.

Gamewright (Division of Ceaco, Inc.)

Gayla Industries, Inc.

Gemmy Industries Corporation

General Creation, Inc.

Gerber Products Company

Global Toys, Inc.

GnuGames, Inc.

Goetz Dolls, Inc.

Goldberger Doll Mfg. Co., Inc.

Good Stuff Corporation

Grand Toys International, Inc.

Great American Puzzle Factory, Inc.

Great American Trading Company

Gund, Inc.

Handi-Craft Company

Hasbro, Inc.

Hedstrom Corporation (Corporate Office)

Hero Factory, Inc.

Highlights for Children, Inc.

Hoberman Designs, Inc.

Home Inspirations, Ltd.

Hong Kong City Toys Factory Ltd.

IDEO, Skyline Studio

Ideoplastos, Inc.

Imperial Toy Corp.

Innovative Kids Children's Books
(Division of Innovative USA)

Insect Lore

International Playthings, Inc.

International Toy Center

International World of Toys

Irwin Toy Limited

ITS - Intertek Testing Services
(Labtest Int'l Division)

J.C. Toys Group, Inc.

JA-RU, Inc.

Jada Toys, Inc.

Jax Ltd., Inc.

Jellycat, Inc.

Jerry Elsner Company, Inc.

The Jester & Pharley Phund

Johnson Research & Development Co., Inc.

K & M International, Inc.

K'NEX Industries, Inc.

K-Group Industries, L.L.C.

Kellytoy (USA), Inc.

KETTLER International, Inc.

Keys Publishing Co, Inc.

Kid Galaxy, Inc.

Kidkraft, L.P.

Kidpower, Inc.

KidzBUILT, L.L.C.

Knowledge Universe, L.L.C.

Koplow Games

Lagoon Games

Laura Tomasetti & Associates Public Relations

Lauri, Inc.

Leannie Company Limited

LeapFrog Enterprises, Inc.

Learning Curve International

The Learning Journey International, L.L.C.

Lee Middleton Original Dolls, Inc.

LEGO Systems, Inc.

Leisure Learning Products/Mighty Mind Kids

Lenson Enterprises

Les Friedland Associates Ltd.

LGB of America, Inc.

Life of the Party, L.L.C.

Life-Like Products, L.L.C.

Lights, Camera, Interaction!, Inc.

Lionel, L.L.C.

Little Kids, Inc.

The Little Tikes Company

Lloyd Middleton's Royal Vienna Doll Collection

Lucky Plastics Factory, Ltd.

Mag-Nif, Inc.

Maisto International, Inc.

Manhattan Toy

Manley Toy Quest

Maple Landmark, Inc.

The Marketing Store

Marklin, Inc.

Marlon Creations

Marvel Enterprises, Inc. (Toy Biz Division)

Mary Meyer Corporation

Mattel, Inc.

Maui Toys, Inc.

Maxim Enterprise, Inc.

Maya Group, Inc.

McGraw-Hill Children's Publishing

Meade Instruments Corp.

MEGA BLOKS (Ritvik Holdings)

Meyer/Glass Design Ltd. Partnership

ML J, Inc.

Mongo Toys, L.L.C.

Monogram International, Inc.

Moon Products, Inc.

MTL- ACTS, Bureau Veritas Consumer
Products Services

Munchkin, Inc.

Namkung Promotions, Inc.

Nanomuscle, Inc.

Natural Science Industries, Ltd.

Neurosmith

New Tech Kites

New-Ray Toys (California), Inc.

Nextoy

Nikko America, Inc.

NuArts Creation, Inc. (Three Heart)

Ohio Art Company

Omega Toy Corp.

Omniglow Corporation

Oregon Scientific, Inc.

P & M Products USA, Inc. (COLORWORKSHOP)

P. J. Kids

Paragon Packaging, Inc.

Parris Manufacturing Company

Patch Products, Inc.

Pebeo of America

Peg Perego U.S.A., Inc.

Peponi International

Plastwood Corporation

Play Along, Inc.

Playing Mantis, Inc.

Playmates Toys, Inc.

Playmobil U.S.A., Inc.

Polyform Products Co., Inc.

Preferred Plush

Premier Kites (Division of Primus)

Pressman Toy Corporation

Prestige Toy Corporation

Prime Time Toys, L.L.C.

Prismatech Publishing, L.L.C.

Processed Plastic Company

PW Resources

Quincrafts Corporation

Radica USA Ltd.

Radio Flyer

Ravensburger-F.X. Schmid USA, Inc.

RBI Toys, Inc.

The Reader's Digest Association, Inc.

Reeves International, Inc.

Regent Products Corp.

Reiner Associates, Inc.

Reprint Mint, Inc.

Reuben Klamer/Toylab

Rocket USA, Inc.

Rokenbok Toy Co.

Rose Art Industries, Inc.

Roylco, Inc.

Rubie's Costumes Company, Inc.

Russ Berrie & Co., Inc.

S.R.M. Entertainment, Ltd.

Sababa Toys, Inc.

Safari Limited

Salo Ventures, L.L.C.

Schoenhut Toy Piano Company, Inc.

Scientific Explorer

Scratch-Art Company, Inc.

Screenlife, L.L.C.

Sesame Workshop

Seymour Mann, Inc.

SGS U.S. Testing Co., Inc.

Shelcore, Inc.

Shure Products, Inc.

Silverlit Toys (USA), Inc.

Simba Toys USA, Inc.

Small Fry Design, Inc.

Small Fry Productions

Small World Toys

Smethport Specialty Company

SnowDroid Industries, Inc.

Sophia's Heritage Collection

Soundprints

Specialized Technology Resources, Inc.

Speedball Art Products, L.L.C.

Spin Master Toys

Sport-Fun, Inc.

Spring Swings, Inc.

Squire Boone Village dba Earth Exploration Co.

The Straight Edge, Inc.

Strombecker Corp.

Sunnywood, Inc.

Superflight, Inc.

Susan Wakeen, Inc.

T-N-T International, Inc. ("Toys-N-Things")

Taiyo Edge Ltd. Co.

Takara U.S.A. Corp.

Tangent Toy Co.

Tangle, Inc.

Team Concepts North America, Ltd.

Techno Mind Ltd., Inc.

Tek-Nek Toys International Ltd.

The Testor Corporation

Texas Popguns

Thomas Boland & Co., Inc.

TMI Toymarketing International, Inc.

Tomy Corporation

Totsy Manufacturing Company, Inc.

ToySite

Trendmasters, Inc.

Uncle Milton Industries, Inc.

Union Wadding Company

USAOPOLY

The Vogue Doll Company, Inc.

V Tech Electronics North America, L.L.C.

Well Made Toy Mfg. Corp.

Westminster, Inc.

What Kids Want, Inc.

Wild Planet Toys, Inc.

Wildlife Artists, Inc.

Winning Moves, Inc.

Wizkids, L.L.C.

Yottoy Productions, Inc.

Zapf Creation U.S.A., Inc.

Zocker Toys

TIA Member Companies as of 10/14/02

Sponsor Companies

The publication of this book would not have been possible without the financial support of our sponsors:

PLATINUM

Fisher-Price Brands

Hasbro, Inc.

K'NEX Industries, Inc.

Mattel, Inc.

Radio Flyer Inc.

GOLD

LEGO Systems, Inc.

SILVER

Bandai America Inc.

Crayola

Funrise Inc.

Hedstrom Corporation

Irwin Toy Limited

LeapFrog Enterprises, Inc.

Learning Curve International

Manhattan Toy

Ohio Art Company

Spin Master Toys

Wild Planet Toys, Inc.

SUPPORTING MEMBERS

Little Kids, Inc.

Meyer/Glass Design Ltd

Silverlit Toys (USA), Inc.

Takara U.S.A. Corp.

Credits

Air Hogs
Courtesy of the 2002 Air Hogs
Summer Van Tour

Baby Alive
Courtesy of Hasbro, Inc.

Barbie Doll
Courtesy of Mattel, Inc.

Bass Fishin'
p. 246 © 2002 Radica USA, Ltd.

Betty Spaghetty
Courtesy of the Ohio Art Company. The Betty Spaghetty® product name is a registered trademark owned by the Ohio Art Company.

Bionicle
LEGO®, the LEGO logo, BIONICLE and the brick configuration are trademarks of the LEGO Group. © 2002 The LEGO Group. LEGO trademarks and images are used with permission.

Brio Wooden Railway
© Brio AB (publ), Sweden 2002

Bubble Mower
p. 216 Courtesy of Fisher-Price, Inc.

Cabbage Patch Kids
Courtesy of Original Appalachian Artworks, Inc.

Candy Land
Courtesy of Hasbro, Inc.

Care Bears®
© 2003 Those Characters From Cleveland, Inc.

Chatter Telephone
Courtesy of Fisher-Price, Inc.

Chatty Cathy
p. 139 Courtesy of Mattel, Inc.

Cherry Twins
p. 127 Walter Pfeiffer from Madame Alexander Dolls: An American Legend © Portfolio Press Corporation

Colorforms
© University Games Corporation, San Francisco, CA 94110

Clue
Photographs by Richard Bachmann

Cootie
p. 94 bottom Courtesy of Macy's.
p. 95 Courtesy of Hasbro, Inc.

Cozy Coupe
© 2002 The Little Tikes Company, Hudson, OH 44236

Crayola Crayons
Photographs provided by and reproduced with permission of Binney & Smith. Photograph of advertisement courtesy of A Century of Crayola® Collectibles, A Price Guide by Bonnie Rushlow. Published by Hobby House Press, Inc.

Doctor and Nurse Kits
© 2002 Pressman Toy Corporation

Doll House
Courtesy of the Museum of the City of New York. Used with permission.

Easy-Bake Oven
p. 156 Photograph by Richard Bachmann
p. 157 Courtesy of Hasbro, Inc.

Erector Set
p. 38 Willard R. Culver/National Geographic Image Collection, 1947

Etch A Sketch
p. 145 Ziggy © 1996 Ziggy and Friends, Inc. Reprinted with permission of Universal Press Syndicate. All rights reserved.
p. 144 Courtesy of the Ohio Art Company. The Etch A Sketch® product name and the configuration of the Etch A Sketch® product are registered trademarks owned by the Ohio Art Company.

FDNY Engine Co. No. 68
Courtesy Code 3 Collectibles

Ford Model T Diecast Car
p. 30 Courtesy of Ford Motor Co.
p. 31 © 2002 Mark Rich

Frisbee
Courtesy of Wham-O

Furby
Courtesy of Hasbro, Inc.

G.I. Joe
pp. 158-159, 161 Copyright 2002 Vincent Santelmo, author, The Complete Encyclopedia to GI Joe. Vincent Santelmo, POB 789, New York, NY 10021 (718) 747-6610.
pp. 160 Courtesy of Hasbro, Inc.

Ginny Dolls
Courtesy of Vogue Doll Co. and Peggy Millhouse

Gooey Louie
© 2002 Pressman Toy Corporation

Groovy Girls
Photographs by Joseph Mulligan

Gumby®
Gumby® images courtesy of Clokey Productions Pokey photograph by Joseph Mulligan

Hot Wheels Cars
Photographs by Brian McCarty, Mattel, Inc.

Hula Hoop
Courtesy of Wham-O

Humpty Dumpty Circus
p. 17 © The Children's Museum of Indianapolis
pp. 16, 18-19 Courtesy of Judy Sneed, Judy's Old Wood Toys, www.oldwoodtoys.com

K'NEX Ferris Wheel
© K'NEX Industries, Inc.

LeapPad
© LeapFrog Enterprises, Inc.

LEGO
LEGO®, the LEGO logo and the brick configuration are trademarks of the LEGO Group. © 2002 The LEGO Group. LEGO trademarks and images are used with permission.

Lincoln Logs
p. 44 Courtesy of Hasbro, Inc.

Lionel Trains
p. 22 Courtesy Barnes & Noble Publishing
p. 22 bottom www.billmilne.com
p. 23-25 Compliments of Lionel

Lite Brite
Courtesy of Hasbro, Inc.

Little People
Courtesy of Fisher-Price, Inc.

Littles Playtime Pals
Lamaze®

Magic 8 Ball
Photograph by Joseph Mulligan

Marbles
p. 50 left Marbles Champ printed by permission of the Norman Rockwell Family Agency.
© 1939 the Norman Rockwell Family Entities

Masters of the Universe
Courtesy of Mattel, Inc.

Matchbox Cars
p. 112 bottom Courtesy of Mattel, Inc.
Other photographs by Richard Bachmann

Mighty Morphin Power Rangers
™ and © BVS Entertainment, Inc., and BVS International N.V. All rights reserved.

Minnie Mouse & Mickey Mouse Dolls
Courtesy of the Walt Disney Company

Monopoly
pp. 72-73 Courtesy of Hasbro, Inc.
p. 74 Courtesy of Forbes Magazine Gallery

Mousetrap
p. 155 Photograph by Joseph Mulligan

Mr. Machine
p. 140 © 2002 Mark Rich

Mr. Potato Head
Courtesy of Hasbro, Inc.

Music Blocks
p. 265 Courtesy of Neurosmith

My Buddy
Courtesy of Hasbro, Inc.

My Little Pony
Courtesy of Hasbro, Inc.

Nerf
p. 179 Christine Polomsky, F+W Publications, Inc. (2001)

Nok-Hockey®
Courtesy of Carrom Company

Play-Doh
Courtesy of Hasbro, Inc.

Playmobil
With kind permission of Geobra Brandstatter GmbH & Co. KG, under which the displayed Playmobil toy figures are also protected

Polly Pocket!
Photographs by Joseph Mulligan

Poo-Chi
The Arizona Republic, 2000, Cheryl Evans. Used with permission. Permission does not imply endorsement.

Radio Flyer
Courtesy of Radio Flyer, Inc.

Raggedy Ann & Raggedy Andy
p. 43 Photograph by David J. Opdyke
Dolls from the collection of Tom and Joni Gruelle Wannamaker and the Johnny Gruelle Raggedy Ann and Andy Museum, Arcola, Illinois
© Simon & Schuster, Inc. Licensed by U. M. Copyright and trademark belong to the Gruelle family, but are controlled by Simon & Schuster.

Rebound
Courtesy of Mattel, Inc.

Red Trike
p. 100 Photograph by Joseph Carapellucci.
© 2003 Carapellucci Design. Reproduced with permission. All rights reserved.
p. 101 © Hedstrom Corp.

Rescue Heroes
Courtesy of Fisher-Price, Inc.

Roy Rogers Cap Pistol
p. 108 Photograph by Joseph Mulligan

Rubik's Cube
Christine Polomsky, F+W Publications, Inc. (2001)

Scrabble
Photograph by Joseph Mulligan

See 'n Say
Courtesy of Fisher-Price, Inc.

Shirley Temple Doll
p. 70 Leonard McCombe/TimePix
p. 71 Collection of Suzanne Kraus-Mancuso

Silly Putty
Photographs provided by and reproduced with permission of Binney & Smith.

Simon
Courtesy of Hasbro, Inc.

Snoopy Sniffer
Courtesy of Fisher-Price, Inc.

Spirograph
p. 172 Photograph by Richard Bachmann
p. 173 Courtesy of Hasbro, Inc.

Spy Vision Goggles™ toy
© Wild Planet Toys

Star Wars Figures
Christine Polomsky, F+W Publications, Inc. (2001)

Strawberry Shortcake
Strawberry Shortcake® toys and other Strawberry Shortcake™ products: © 2003 Those Characters From Cleveland, Inc.

Stretch Armstrong
Courtesy of Hasbro, Inc.

Talking Barney
Barney © 1992 Lyons Partnership, L. P. Used with permission.

Teddy Bear
p. 26 National Museum of American History, Smithsonian Institution, Behring Center
p. 27 (c) 1902, The Washington Post. Reprinted with permission.

Teddy Ruxpin
Christine Polomsky, F+W Publications, Inc. (2001)

Teenage Mutant Ninja Turtles
© Lee Publications 2002

Tickle Me Elmo
Courtesy of Fisher-Price, Inc.

Tinkertoy
p. 41 Courtesy of Hasbro, Inc.

Tonka Mighty Dump Truck
Photograph by Richard Bachmann

Transformers
Courtesy of Hasbro, Inc.

Trivial Pursuit
p. 204 Photograph by Richard Bachmann
p. 205 Courtesy of Hasbro, Inc.

Trolls
p. 136 Ralph Morse/TimePix
p. 137 © Russ Berrie and Company, Inc., Oakland, NJ

Tuneyville Choo-Choo
© 1998 Tomy Corporation

Twister
p. 170 Photograph by Richard Bachmann
p. 171 Courtesy of Hasbro, Inc.

View-Master
p. 78 top Courtesy of Fisher-Price, Inc.
p. 78 bottom Photograph by Mark Rich

Wonder Spring Horse
Wonder® by Hedstrom®

Yo-Yo
p. 59 Lucky's Collectors Guide to 20th Century Yo-Yos

Zolo
© Zolo, Inc. Zolo is a registered trademark of Higashi Glaser Design.

FRONT COVER
Clockwise from 1903 (top):

Ford Model T Die-cast car
Photograph by Richard Bachmann

Raggedy Ann & Raggedy Andy dolls
David J. Opdyke

Liberty Coaster wagon
Courtesy of Radio Flyer, Inc.

Duncan Yo-yo
Courtesy of Flambeau Products Corporation

Shirley Temple doll
Collection of Suzanne Kraus-Mancuso

View Master
Courtesy of Fisher-Price, Inc.

Mr. Potato Head
Courtesy of Hasbro, Inc.

Slinky

Barbie doll
Courtesy of Mattel, Inc.

Etch A Sketch
Courtesy of the Ohio Art Company

G.I. Joe
Courtesy of Hasbro, Inc.

Cozy Coupe
Courtesy of The Little Tikes Company

Mighty Morphin Power Ranger
Courtesy of BVS Entertainment, Inc. and BVS International N.V.

LeapPad
Courtesy of LeapFrog Enterprises, Inc.

Groovy Girl figure
Courtesy of Manhattan Toy

Fisher-Price, Little People, Rescue Heroes, See 'n Say, View-Master, Chatter Telephone, Bubble Mower, Snoopy Sniffer and related trademarks and copyrights are used with permission from Fisher-Price.

HASBRO and its logo, BABY ALIVE, CANDY LAND, COOTIE, EASY-BAKE, FURBY, G.I. JOE, LINCOLN LOGS, LITE-BRITE, MONOPOLY, MOUSETRAP, MR. POTATO HEAD, MY LITTLE PONY, PLAY-DOH, POO-CHI, RAGGEDY ANDY, RAGGEDY ANN, SIMON, SPIROGRAPH, STRETCH ARMSTRONG, TINKERTOY, TONKA, TRANSFORMERS and TWISTER are trademarks of Hasbro and are used with permission.
© 2002 Hasbro.
All rights reserved.
RAGGEDY ANN and RAGGEDY ANDY were created by Johnny Gruelle.
SCRABBLE is a trademark of Hasbro in the U.S. and Canada. © 2002 Hasbro, Inc.
All rights reserved.
TRIVIAL PURSUIT is a registered trademark of Horn Abbot Ltd. used in connection with games distributed and sold in the U.S. under exclusive license to Hasbro, Inc.

BARBIE® is a trademark owned by and used with the permission of Mattel, Inc. © 2002 Mattel, Inc. All rights reserved.
CHATTY CATHY® is a trademark owned by and used with the permission of Mattel, Inc. © 2002 Mattel, Inc. All rights reserved.
MAGIC 8 BALL® is a trademark owned by and used with the permission of Mattel, Inc. © 2002 Mattel, Inc. All rights reserved.
ROCK 'EM SOCK 'EM™ is a trademark owned by and used with the permission of Mattel, Inc. © 2002 Mattel, Inc. All rights reserved.

HISTORY
p. 82 middle TimePix
p. 83 middle Courtesy Randy Inman Auctions
p. 118 left TimePix
p. 118 bottom Armstrong Roberts/Retrofile
p. 119 top left, 150 top, 182 top, 208 top TimePix
p. 234 Benjamin Bodnar, Junior Skateboarding Park Final, 2002 Asian X-Games Qualifier, Kuala Lumpur, Malaysia, 2002, Stanley Chou/Getty Images

Hulton Archive/Getty Images
Pages 12, 14 bottom, 15, 28, 32, 34 middle & bottom, 35, 40, 42, 50 top, 52-58, 66-69, 80-81 top, 83 top & bottom, 100 right, 109, 116-117 top & left, 119 bottom left, 148-150 middle & bottom, 151 top left & bottom right, 178, 180 , 183 top, 206, 208 bottom, 209 bottom right, 217, 234, 236 bottom, 237 bottom & left, 247, 264.

Author
Chris Byrne

Author
Chris Byrne

Chris Byrne is one of the leading experts on children's toys, lifestyle trends and play in the U.S. today. A twenty-four-year veteran of the toy industry, Byrne, also known as "The Toy Guy,"™ is sought out regularly by the media to discuss the international business of the children's entertainment industries. A contributing editor to *The Toy Book*, editor of *The Toy Report*, contributing editor to *Toy Wishes Magazine* and a social and cultural historian focusing on toys and play, Byrne also consults for leading Fortune 100 companies on play trends and children's lifestyle patterns. He appears regularly on television worldwide and his choice tips for caregivers and product reviews can be found on thetoyguy.com and eBay.com, as well as in various other publications around the globe.